PROFESSIONAL RECORDS AND INFORMATION MANAGEMENT

SECOND EDITION

Jeffrey R. Stewart

Nancy M. Melesco

Glencoe
McGraw-Hill

New York, New York   Columbus, Ohio   Woodland Hills, California   Peoria, Illinois

Glencoe/McGraw-Hill

A Division of The **McGraw·Hill** Companies

Professional Records and Information Management

Send all inquiries to:

Glencoe/McGraw-Hill
21600 Oxnard Street, Suite 500
Woodland Hills, CA 91367-4947

ISBN-13: 978-0-07-822779-0
ISBN-10: 0-07-822779-8

Printed in the United States of America.

6 7 8 9 0   DOCDOC   0109876

REVIEWERS

The authors, editor, and publisher recognize the following reviewers for their valuable contributions to the development of this book.

Murlene Asadi
Department Chair—Administrative and
	Office Support Programs
Scott Community College
Davenport, Iowa

Jennie A. Dehn
Instructor
Bryant & Stratton
Buffalo, New York

Terri A. DeWerff
Campus Director
Sanford Brown College
Granite City, Illinois

Terri Gonzales
Instructor, Business Studies
Delgado Community College
New Orleans, Louisiana

Joyce Gronroos
Instructor
Santa Rosa Junior College, Petaluma Campus
Petaluma, California

Barb Kaldenberger
Office Technology Instructor
Blackhawk Technical College
Janesville, Wisconsin

Carol Y. Mull
Chairperson, Computer Technologies
Ashville-Buncombe Technical Community
	College
Ashville, North Carolina

Jane M. Pendry
Guilford Technical Community College
Jamestown, North Carolina

Janice A. Rowland
Associate Professor
Pellissippi State Technical Community College
Knoxville, Tennessee

Jean Shull
St. Louis Community College—Meramec
St. Louis, Missouri

Brenda A. Smith
Academic Division Chair
State Technical Institute at Memphis
Memphis, Tennessee

Ramona S. Stephens
Associate Professor
Northeast State Technical Community College
Blountville, Tennessee

Dr. Melba Taylor
Professor of Administrative Support
	Technology
Virginia Highlands Community College
Abingdon, Virginia

Nancy Vrieze
Business Instructor
Wisconsin Indianhead Technical College
Rice Lake, Wisconsin

Sharon Werner
Instructor, Business Division
Pierce College
Lakewood, Washington

Debbie West, CPS
Dean of Students
Draughons Junior College
Nashville, Tennessee

ACKNOWLEDGMENT

The authors recognize Stephen Williams, an independent consultant, for his contributions in planning and preparing Chapters 8, 9, and 10 and for updating the database project in the practice materials.

CONTENTS

PREFACE		vi
UNIT 1	**The Profession of Records and Information Management**	2
Chapter 1	Introduction to Records and Information Management	4
Chapter 2	Employment in Records and Information Management	14
Chapter 3	Legal and Ethical Matters in Records and Information Management	22
	Professional Activities for Unit 1 (Chapters 1–3)	30
UNIT 2	**Managing Nonelectronic Records**	32
Chapter 4	Receipt and Creation of Hard Copy Records	34
Chapter 5	Indexing and Alphabetizing Procedures	46
Chapter 6	Systems for Organizing Paper Records	66
Chapter 7	Retrieval, Retention, and Recycling	86
	Professional Activities for Unit 2 (Chapters 4–7)	98
UNIT 3	**Electronic Information Management**	100
Chapter 8	Managing Electronic Files	102
Chapter 9	Using Electronic Databases	128
Chapter 10	Network-Based Records Management	152
Chapter 11	Image Technology and Automated Systems	178
Chapter 12	Safety, Security, and Disaster Recovery	198
	Professional Activities for Unit 3 (Chapters 8–12)	214
APPENDIX A	**Additional Indexing and Alphabetizing Practice**	216
APPENDIX B	**Professional Associations**	220
APPENDIX C	**Professional Publications**	222
KEYS	**Keys for Chapter 5 and Appendix A**	224
GLOSSARY		231
INDEX		243

Professional Records and Information Management is a careful revision of the successful edition titled *Professional Records Management*. The term *information* was added to the title to acknowledge the dramatic growth of information technology, especially as it relates to the use of computers, databases, and networks for managing information.

Records and information management (RIM) is increasingly being recognized as a profession in and of itself. The recent emergence of the corporate title chief information officer, or CIO, testifies to the growing status of the field. Overseeing the billions of records produced each day requires professional experience and commitment. The professional records manager or information manager may or may not have the title of records manager or information manager. Still, all who work with records must be adept in and knowledgeable about the profession of records and information management, the management of nonelectronic records and information, and electronic information management. This text is organized into three units; each addresses one of those crucial ingredients of records and information management.

Unit 1, The Profession of Records and Information Management, introduces basic terminology and discusses the scope of records and information management, employment opportunities, and legal and ethical matters associated with records and information management. Unit 2, Managing Nonelectronic Records, considers the life cycle of hard copy records and the indexing protocols required to organize records. Unit 3, Electronic Information Management, has been completely reworked in this edition. This unit is a comprehensive introduction to current developments in electronic information management. Topics include electronic computer filing systems, database systems, image technology, and automated systems used to manage paper records. A completely new chapter in Unit 3 is Chapter 10, Network-Based Records Management. This new chapter deals with e-mail, the Internet, and related topics so vital to the management of information today. Each of the three units begins with a profile of a real-life RIM professional and concludes with realistic application activities that provide practice in managing records of all types.

Filing and Computer Database Projects

The practice set for this text is titled *Filing and Computer Database Projects*. It includes both manual and computer database simulations. The manual part of the practice set includes alphabetic, numeric, geographic, and subject filing of names and data that are used later in the computer database part of the set. The manual portion also includes decision-making activities in the creation, receipt, storage, and retention of correspondence and other realistic documents.

In the computer database part of the practice set, the user works with a customer database, a client database, and an inventory database—each in the context of a simulated business. In addition, the user designs and creates a small employee database.

Other Supporting Materials

Filing Rules Tutorial

The CD inside the back cover of this textbook contains a stand-alone filing rules tutorial of eight to twelve hours of alphabetic filing practice using the twelve filing rules. Its use is intended to reinforce the work in Chapter 5. Instructions for using the CD appear on page 250.

Gregg Quick Filing Practice

A popular alternative to *Filing and Computer Database Projects* is *Gregg Quick Filing Practice*. This boxed set provides approximately twenty hours of manual filing practice.

Your Challenge and Your Opportunity

By carefully studying the material in this book and completing the activities in the practice set, you will be well on your way to great opportunities and challenges in records and information management. This growing profession requires more and more dedicated and knowledgeable professionals. Your challenge is to grasp the opportunity to join their ranks.

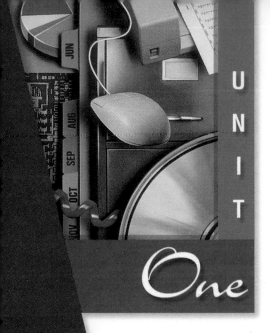

The Profession of Records and Information Management

Unit 1 is an overview of the profession of records and information management (RIM). You will learn what RIM is, its functions, and its employment opportunities and be introduced to some of the major professional organizations in RIM. Finally, you will consider legal and ethical concerns that confront the records and information management professional.

PROFESSIONAL PROFILE

PATRICIA CONNELLY
Glen Allen, Virginia

Meet Patricia Connelly. Patricia is an Information Technology Operations Associate at Capital One Financial Corporation. Her job is to maintain the documentation library. Patricia's responsibilities include maintaining an up-to-date filing system, making sure all documentation is completed in hard copy packets with required signatures, filing and tracking the documentation, ensuring that proper retention procedures are in place, and developing new methods for tracking documentation. Her job requires strong organizational skills, good communication and interpersonal skills, and skill in word processing and spreadsheet applications. In addition, Patricia has to be creative, resourceful, and detail-oriented to properly maintain all the records.

Patricia's Career Path. Patricia refined her organizational skills from previous work experiences. She has held her current position for 1-1/2 years and hopes one day to move up to manager of the documentation staff. Her experience plus the two-year degree she is working toward at J. Sargent Reynolds Community College will prepare her for that move.

Introduction to Records and Information Management

The purpose of Chapter 1 is to enable you to:

- **Define records and information management (RIM).**
- **Recognize the functions of records and information management and the steps in the life cycle of records.**
- **Identify employment opportunities in both the private and public sectors that require records and information management expertise.**

KEY TERMS

- contract
- hard copy
- information system
- nonrecord
- record
- records and information management

Most private and public sector organizations depend on information to operate. For example, to do business, a company must have information about its:

- Customers
- Suppliers
- Employees

How businesses and other organizations plan, develop, and organize their information is called their **information system**. Some information, such as job applications and minutes of board meetings, is recorded on paper (**hard copy**). Other information is recorded on computer disks or hard drives, microfilm, or other media. Inventory records, for example, are often kept in a computer *database,* which is a collection of related files that support a business or organization. Regardless of the medium, **records and information management (RIM)** deals with the creation, distribution, maintenance, protection, control, storage, and eventual destruction of business and organization records.

Identifying a Record

A **record** is a piece of information created by or received by an organization or business that gives evidence of a business decision or transaction and should be preserved. Some records are kept because of government regulations. Other records are retained as proof of what was decided or agreed upon in business transactions. Businesses are flooded with information; it is not desirable or cost-effective to keep all of it. RIM professionals have the responsibility of deciding what is a **record** and what is a **nonrecord**.

Most **contracts** are records of vital importance to an organization. A contract is an agreement, usually in writing, between two parties that sets forth the expectations for each side. If there is a dispute between the parties, a copy of the contract will be needed to prove the original intent so that the contract can be upheld. Patents, stock purchases, and sales data are other examples of records that organizations should retain.

A nonrecord is a document that is more expensive to keep than to discard. For example, keeping copies of order acknowledgments sent to customers usually costs more than they are worth. In the 1990s, some tobacco companies maintained records that could have been destroyed legally but were kept and later used against them.

Identifying Documents

Record
A piece of information created or received by an organization that should be preserved.

Nonrecord
A document that is more expensive to keep than to discard.

Records and Information Management Functions

In your study of records and information management, you will become familiar with the functions of *RIM*. A brief description of each function follows.

Creation

A records and information manager must consider factors such as cost, format, medium, and accessibility before records are created. For example, if the cost of creating a record is greater than its value to a business, the record probably should not be created at all.

Functions of RIM

Creating, distributing, maintaining, protecting, controlling, storing, and eventually destroying the records created in an information system.

Distribution

Distribution is the act of delivering a record to an individual who has a need to see the information contained in the record. Should a paper record be created in four copies? Who will use each copy, and for what purpose? How are the copies to be sent to the users? Choices of delivery include fax machine, mail, interoffice delivery, or electronic mail. Questions such as those listed above must be considered before records are distributed.

Maintenance

The records and information manager is responsible for maintaining the *integrity* of the organization's records **(Figure 1.1)**. As used here, integrity refers to records being current, accurate, and relevant to the operation. For example, for a payroll to be accurate, the employees who prepare the payroll must have accurate and up-to-date information about the pay rate of each worker.

Protection

Protection includes keeping records safe and secure—safe from physical hazards, such as fire and floods, and secure to maintain the privacy of the records **(Figure 1.2)**.

Figure 1.1

A record must be maintained for safe-keeping and easy retrieval. *Which phase is this in the life cycle of a record?*

Figure 1.2

Records must be protected from natural and human disasters as well as theft and sabotage. Protection is the fourth phase in the life cycle of a record. *How would you protect the records in your private files?*

Control

The records and information manager must *control*, or regulate, the use of records within the organization. Only authorized persons should have access to records. Records that are borrowed must also be controlled. Controlling borrowed records includes documenting the records that are borrowed, who is borrowing them, when they are borrowed, and when they are due back. It also includes tracking, or following up, to make sure they are returned on time.

Storage

Records must be preserved, or *stored*, so they can be found when needed **(Figure 1.3).**

Inactive or historical records must be stored in a safe place and organized for rapid retrieval if needed.

Figure 1.3

Storage is the sixth phase in the life cycle of a record. *When might a record be stored in another location?*

Destruction

The records and information manager is responsible for determining when records should be destroyed and overseeing their destruction. Records can be destroyed when they are no longer needed in the operations of the organization or when they are no longer required for legal reasons **(Figure 1.4)**. The manager must make decisions concerning how to recycle records as part of the environmental protection policies of the organization.

Figure 1.4

The seventh phase in the life cycle of a record is its destruction. A record is destroyed or recycled when it no longer has value to the organization. *How would you describe a valuable record?*

Life Cycle of Records

- Creation
- Distribution
- Maintenance
- Protection
- Control
- Storage
- Destruction

Life Cycle of Records

The functions described above, when they are tied together, can be looked upon as steps in the life cycle of records, as shown in **Figure 1.5**. As shown in the diagram, records are first created, then distributed to users. Next, records are maintained on a day-to-day basis. They are protected and controlled while being used. Records are stored and sometimes transferred to inactive storage near the end of the life cycle. Finally, when they are no longer of value to the organization, the records are destroyed and in many cases recycled to protect the environment.

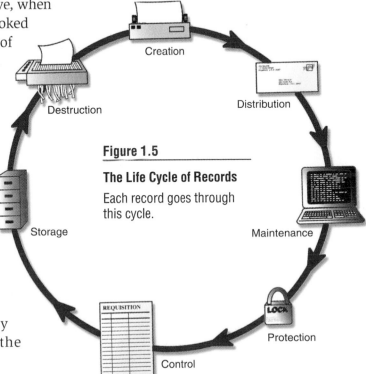

Creation

Destruction

Distribution

Figure 1.5

The Life Cycle of Records
Each record goes through this cycle.

Storage

Maintenance

Protection

Control

The Professional Records and Information Manager

Many businesses and organizations employ or contract with records and information management professionals. Job titles include chief information officer (CIO), records manager, records and information manager, and records and information management consultant. These individuals often have a two- or four-year college major in one of the business disciplines or in information and library science. In addition, they usually have experience in managing information and records. Many belong to professional organizations such as the Association of Records Managers and Administrators, Inc. The professional records and information manager is responsible for planning and implementing an organization-wide program that encompasses all records and information functions.

Records Management Field

RIM AS A PROFESSION. The RIM professional is important to the success of many organizations. Numerous administrative, fiscal, and managerial jobs also require a basic knowledge of RIM. Other professions whose members should have a foundation in RIM are accountant, office manager, branch manager, department head, administrative assistant, executive assistant, legal assistant, medical assistant, marketing manager, and marketing assistant.

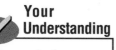

Your Understanding

What are the functions of RIM?

In summary, the field of records and information management includes two groups: (1) specialists in RIM and (2) employees whose occupation includes the management of information but who have another specialty or job title. Professionals in both groups make decisions that affect the life cycle of records. They all deal with the important functions of the emerging field of records and information management.

Look at the daily schedule of a RIM professional, Douglas Toussant, the records and information manager for a large law firm, Sager, Haart, and Donnovan, PC. The schedule shown on page 11 is an example of one day's activities and projects. It gives you some idea of the variety of Toussant's daily activities—working with people, ideas, technology, and resources.

A Day in the Life of a Records Professional

Sager, Haart, and Donnovan, PC
Douglas Toussant, Records and Information Manager
Schedule for Thursday, March 18, 20—

Time	Planned Projects and Activities
8 A.M.	Assemble cost figures for 9 A.M. meeting with controller. Expenditures will be used to convert paper case files in folders and cabinets to optical disk case files for the new information management system.
9 A.M.	Meet with controller to discuss possible increase in equipment and staffing budget in next fiscal year.
10 A.M.	Interview Paula Salera, candidate for systems analyst position, who will be responsible for setting up and providing database maintenance for the new optical disk case files.
11 A.M.	Write standards for entering data (case files) into the computer system.
12 noon	ARMA local chapter meeting/luncheon at Holiday House Inn and Conference Center. Speaker topic: Internet Challenges.
1:30 P.M.	Meet with Jun Chen, Indus-Star bar code scanner salesperson, to see if this product meets standards for entering data into the computer system.
2 P.M.	Conduct training session for partners on how they might use the new computer case file system and how to deal with transition procedures. See PowerPoint file CASE.PTT and COMPCASE.RIM for notes and visuals.
3 P.M.	Training session in progress until 4 P.M.
4 P.M.	Send e-mail to partners thanking them for attending and providing suggestions in today's training session. Include list of suggestions given and assure them that each will be considered for incorporation in the new computer system.
5 P.M.	Meet with records and information management staff regarding progress in preparing to phase in the new information management system.
6 P.M.	Phone Sam Carruthers, RIM consultant in California (415-555-3280). Ask him if he will be able to meet on April 6 to provide technical advice on bar code input.

TERMS TO KNOW

▼

1. Review these key terms and important terms.

- **contract**
- **control**
- **database**
- **hard copy**
- **information system**
- **integrity**
- **nonrecord**

- **protection**
- **record**
- **records and information management**
- **RIM**
- **stored**

2. Match a term from the above list to each of these definitions.

- How businesses and other organizations plan, develop, and organize their information.
- A document that is more expensive to keep than to discard.
- An agreement between two parties, usually in writing.
- Paper record.
- The creation, distribution, maintenance, protection, control, storage, and eventual destruction of business and organization records.
- Information created or received that should be preserved.

DISCUSSION QUESTIONS

▼

Answer each question as a written assignment or for class discussion. Be concise in your responses.

1. Give some examples of important records that an organization might keep.
2. Define *information system.*
3. What functions are part of *records and information management*?
4. Should cost be considered in the creation of a record? Why? What kinds of costs might be incurred?
5. Explain the meaning of integrity in relation to the maintenance function of RIM.

6. What is the main concern in the storage function of RIM?

7. What are two situations in which records might be destroyed?

8. When all the functions of RIM are tied together, what can they be viewed as?

CRITICAL THINKING

Think for Yourself The purposes of these end-of-chapter activities are to help you think creatively and reason logically. Follow three general guidelines to careful thinking: (1) gather and evaluate facts and ideas relative to the problem or situation, (2) generalize from the facts and ideas, and (3) create new ideas from available data and your own experience. Follow your instructor's directions as to whether to work independently or as a member of a group.

1. **Gather Facts** Arrange an interview with two business persons. Ask them what they consider to be the steps in the life cycle of records. Write down their responses, and be careful not to comment positively or negatively on what they say.

2. **Generalize from Facts** Compare the responses from the businesspersons to Figure 1.5 on page 9. Write a statement about (1) how Figure 1.5 might be improved and (2) what factors the businesspersons should consider in the life cycle of records that they did not convey to you.

3. **Create New Ideas** Design a new Figure 1.5 that you believe communicates the concept of the life cycle of records.

NETWORKING WITH THE REAL WORLD

Look for the jobs advertised in your local or regional newspaper. Select a minimum of 3 jobs in which you might be interested. Describe how you might find more information about these jobs.

Employment in Records and Information Management

The purpose of Chapter 2 is to enable you to:

- Classify and describe specializations in records and information management.
- Identify jobs in both the private and public sectors that require records and information management expertise.
- Describe the type of preparation required for employment in records and information management.
- Explain the importance and advantages of being a member of a professional association.
- Name and briefly describe the purpose of several professional associations for those who work in the field of records and information management.

KEY TERMS

- archival management
- archives
- archivist
- ARMA International
- CRM
- depository
- ICRM
- records center
- SAA

As you learned in Chapter 1, professional records and information managers specialize in RIM. In addition, other professionals have jobs requiring only a basic knowledge of RIM. In this chapter you will look at employment opportunities for both groups. In addition, you will learn about professional RIM associations, their purposes, and the advantages of membership.

Specializations in Records and Information Management

Although there are no clearly defined categories of RIM specialties, the classes of records and employment described in the following sections are generally recognized as requiring unique RIM knowledge and skill.

Archives

Archives are groups of records, usually valuable and historical, that in most cases are not referred to in the day-to-day operations of the organization. They may be kept to meet legal requirements or to maintain important historical facts about the organization. Maintaining archives, or **archival** (pronounced ar-**kī**-vul) **management,** often carries the job title **archivist** (**ar**-kuh-vist). Large organizations, corporations, museums, libraries, and records storage centers are likely to employ archivists. Archivists are often concerned with the long-term maintenance and preservation of all types of records. Many archivists have a background in library and information science or history.

Educational Records

Educational records include information about students, courses taken, credits earned, and test scores. Such records must be maintained so that they can be retrieved many years after a student has left the school system or college.

Financial Records

The person responsible for maintaining financial records frequently has a background in information systems, accounting, or finance. The financial records and information manager is more involved with the daily operations of the business than the archivist. Duties involve designing records systems, updating records, and designing controls to ensure the integrity of all financial records.

Government Records

The management of government records is a specialization that includes local, state, and federal records. The government records manager must be especially aware of safeguarding citizens' rights. In addition to documents pertaining to businesses and individuals, the government records professional is responsible for selecting and retaining historical records.

Legal Records

The legal profession depends heavily on accurate, properly maintained records that can be located when needed. Employment may be with a law firm that is large enough to have its own records professionals. Employment may also be with a governmental unit, such as a city or county, that keeps important legal documents like deeds, wills, birth certificates, marriage records, and tax records. Professionals in legal records management may have a background in government and political science, law, business, or the social sciences.

Medical Records

Perhaps even more important than legal records are medical records. Hospitals, physicians' and dentists' offices, health care agencies, nursing homes, health insurance carriers, and government health agencies rely heavily on accurate medical record keeping. Many of these organizations employ medical records specialists to assist in managing the large volume of medical records. Employees in medical RIM may have a background in business, medical technology, medical records, nursing, insurance, or health care services.

Records Centers and Depositories

Some firms are in the business of managing records for others. Such companies establish records centers and charge a fee for both storage and access. A **records center** is a secure location that is dedicated to the storage of all types of documents and records for various companies and organizations. Some records centers are even located in deep underground caves and caverns to provide additional protection. Many government agencies have special depositories where records are brought for long-term storage. A **depository,** also called *repository,* is a company's or organization's off-site location for housing its records. In both records centers and depositories, other services may be performed, including filming of records,

Specializations in RIM

- Archival management
- Educational records
- Financial records
- Government records
- Legal records
- Medical records
- Records centers and depositories
- Consulting

disaster recovery, and records destruction. Employees are expected to have organizational skills and to work with speed and accuracy in various office and warehouse tasks. The worker may be required to operate highly technical equipment used in converting records from paper form to electronic or photographic images.

Consulting

Business and government records continue to become more numerous, and legal record-keeping requirements become more complex. As a result, more individuals and businesses have turned to professional records and information management consultants. Consultants may perform records surveys and make recommendations for improving records systems. They may be retained by a business to make the necessary changes that will, in turn, make the business's records systems more effective. Consultants are frequently employed by organizations that cannot afford to hire their own full-time records and information specialists. They are also useful to the organization that needs a fresh, outside perspective of its RIM operations. Employment as a consultant requires a detailed knowledge of all phases of records and information management. A college major in information systems, records management, or a related discipline is excellent preparation for a consulting career.

Professional Associations

Professional associations in any field can contribute to the effectiveness of both the profession and those who work in it. Records and information management professionals have realized the value of these dual advantages because the growth of professional associations in RIM has been impressive in recent years. In addition to providing professional identity, unity, and improvement, these associations provide many direct and indirect services to their members. One example of a direct benefit is the trade show, as shown in **Figure 2.1.**

The following sections describe three professional associations for employees in RIM: The Association of Records

Your Understanding

List some RIM specializations.

Figure 2.1

Trade shows are a popular feature at RIM professional association conventions. *How would you find out where trade shows are being held?*

Managers and Administrators, Inc., the Institute of Certified Records Managers, and the Society of American Archivists. See Appendix B for a list of other professional associations.

ARMA International

The Association of Records Managers and Administrators, Inc., also known as **ARMA International** or simply ARMA, "is a not-for-profit association serving more than 10,000 information management professionals in the United States, Canada, and over thirty-five other nations. ARMA International members include records and information managers, MIS and ADP professionals, imaging specialists, archivists, hospital administrators, legal administrators, librarians, and educators" (ARMA International, 1999). More than 150 local ARMA chapters provide networking and leadership opportunities through monthly meetings and special seminars.

ARMA has adopted a mission statement that reflects its professional view of records and information management. Its mission statement follows:

ARMA's mission is:

To provide education, research, and networking opportunities to information professionals, to enable them to use their skills and experience to leverage the value of records, information, and knowledge as corporate assets and contributors to organizational success. *(ARMA International, 1999)*

Your Understanding

What are some advantages of joining a professional association?

Benefits of ARMA Membership

- Continued education
- Networking through industry specific groups
- Technical publications
- *The Information Management Journal*

Membership in ARMA includes opportunities for continued education and professional networking through chapter meetings, local seminars, home study courses, certification study groups, and other exam preparation resources. The organization also hosts an annual conference. It creates opportunities through thirty-four industry specific groups to network with other records professionals working within the same industry. ARMA members have access to technical publications featuring solution-oriented books and visual aids offered at discounted prices. Members also have access to **The Information Management Journal,** the leading professional journal in the records management field.

Institute of Certified Records Managers (ICRM)

ICRM is an "international certifying organization of and for professional records managers" (Institute of Certified Records Managers, 1999). ICRM oversees the professional designation of **certified records manager (CRM).** The CRM designation can be earned by applicants who pass a comprehensive six-part examination and meet work experience certification requirements. In addition, the person holding the CRM designation must maintain certification through approved educational activity.

Society of American Archivists (SAA)

This organization has more than 3600 individual and institutional members who are "concerned with the identification, preservation, and use of records of historical value" (Society of American Archivists, 1999).

Professional Associations

- ARMA
- ICRM
- SAA

CHAPTER 2 REVIEW

TERMS TO KNOW

1. Review these key terms and important terms.

- **achival management**
- **archives**
- **archivist**
- **ARMA International**
- **CRM**
- **depository**
- **ICRM**
- **records center**
- **SAA**

2. Write one or two paragraphs that contain each of the key terms. Underline or italicize each term.

DISCUSSION QUESTIONS

Answer each question as a written assignment or for class discussion. Be concise in your responses.

1. What types of organizations are likely to employ archivists?
2. What are the duties of the person responsible for maintaining financial records?
3. Name several types of legal records that might be kept by a governmental unit such as a city or county.
4. Employees who work in medical RIM might have what type of background?
5. Other than storage and protection of records, what services might be performed by records centers and depositories?
6. Why have more individuals and businesses turned to professional RIM consultants?
7. What is ARMA? What are the benefits of membership?
8. What organization oversees the professional designation CRM?
9. What are some advantages of joining a professional RIM association?

CRITICAL THINKING

1. **Gather Facts**   Determine job opportunities in records and information management in your community or a nearby urban area. Your guidance office, the Internet, the library, and the classified sections of newspapers are all sources of employment information. Prepare a brief written report summarizing the number and kinds of opportunities available, pay, and specific job titles.

2. **Generalize from Facts**   Compare the information about employment in records and information management in Chapter 2 with the information you found. List (1) similarities in the two sources, (2) opportunities you discovered that do not appear in Chapter 2, and (3) opportunities mentioned in Chapter 2 that you did not find. Based on similarities or differences in your research and Chapter 2, make a general statement about the contents of Chapter 2.

3. **Create New Ideas**   For one of the job opportunities you found in Gather Facts, write a letter of application for the position. The letter should have two or three paragraphs and should summarize why you believe you are qualified for the job.

NETWORKING WITH THE REAL WORLD

Access *Resume Writing Center.* The address is http://www.careermosaic.com/cm/rwc. Using this resource as a guide, write a resume for yourself.

Legal and Ethical Matters in Records and Information Management

The purpose of Chapter 3 is to enable you to:

- Distinguish between criminal and civil legal matters.
- Categorize significant federal legislation as relating to business records or government records.
- Discuss civil legal matters that are of importance to RIM employees.
- Evaluate your attitude toward ethical issues in records and information management.

KEY TERMS

- admissibility into evidence
- civil law
- copyright
- criminal law
- litigation
- software piracy

Numerous local, state, and federal government laws and regulations deal with records and information management. Violations of these laws and regulations may be treated as criminal legal matters, or matters covered under **criminal law.** Criminal violations may result in legal action being taken against the violator by the government. Therefore, it is important for the records and information management professional to be familiar with the most important of these laws and regulations.

Employees who are involved with records and information management must also be aware of certain civil legal matters that could affect them or their company. A civil dispute, covered under **civil law,** is a legal disagreement between one person or company and another. For example, a customer might sue your employer because of an injury caused by one of your company's products, in which case the records related to the development and manufacture of that product would be vital in defending your company in court.

As a RIM professional, it is also important that you consider your ethical responsibilities to your employer, your customers, and yourself.

Your Understanding

What is the difference between civil and criminal law?

Government Laws and Regulations

Government laws and regulations related to records and information can be classified into those that deal with:

- How private sector, or business, records are kept.
- How public sector, or government, records are kept.
- The rights and responsibilities of citizens related to records and information.

Laws Dealing with Business Records

Business records from the private sector provide government agencies with much of the information they need to determine if those businesses are complying with the laws and regulations enacted by government for the purpose of

Laws Dealing with Business Records

- Age Discrimination and Employment Act
- Civil Rights Act
- Digital Millennium Copyright Act (DMCA)
- Electronic Communications Privacy Act (ECPA)
- Employee Retirement Income Security Act
- Equal Pay Act
- Fair Labor Standards Act
- Federal Insurance Contributions Act (FICA)
- Federal Unemployment Tax Act (FUTA)
- Occupational Safety and Health Act (OSHA)
- Uniform Photographic Copies of Business and Public Records as Evidence Act (UPA)
- Uniform Rules of Evidence Act

protecting the rights of individuals. For example, the payroll records of a business can be used to verify that employees covered by the federal Fair Labor Standards Act are being paid the minimum wage or more. Several examples of federal laws that specify how business records must be kept or how long they must be retained are listed on page 23.

Laws Dealing with Government Records

Government agencies also keep large volumes of records. Several federal laws regulate how government records are to be kept and for how long. For example, the Paperwork Reduction Act of 1980 is intended to streamline how federal government information is stored by reducing the number and volume of paper records. Several examples of laws that specify how federal government records must be kept or how long they must be retained are listed in the box below.

Laws Dealing with Government Records

- Federal Paperwork Reduction Act of 1980
- Federal Property and Administrative Services Act
- Federal Records Act
- Federal Reports Act
- Records Disposal Act

Your Understanding

How are laws related to records and information classified?

Laws Dealing with Citizens' Rights and Responsibilities

The federal government has recognized the right of citizens to have access to (1) information about the operation of federal government agencies and (2) information on file about themselves. The law that guarantees these rights is the Freedom of Information Act, which was passed in 1966 and amended in 1974.

An individual's right to privacy has also been recognized in federal legislation. The Privacy Act of 1974 denies access to one's personal records without that person's permission.

A **copyright** is an exclusive right granted by the government for the production, publication, or sale of an artistic, musical, or literary work. Copyright laws deal with each person's responsibility to honor ownership of copyrighted works. As a RIM professional, you can duplicate copyrighted items only with permission of the owner or for certain noncommercial "fair use(s)" covered by the law. It is also important to remember that copyright laws prohibit, under most conditions, the duplication of official government items such as paper money, stamps, treasury notes, and savings bonds. The Software Act of 1980 clarifies the fact that computer software is covered by copyright laws. Thus, it is illegal, with certain exceptions, to make duplicates of copyrighted software. The act of duplicating copyrighted software illegally is called **software piracy.**

Your Understanding

What is a copyright?

Civil Legal Concerns

The RIM employee must be aware that civil legal matters often cost as much in time and money as those related to compliance with government laws and regulations (criminal legal matters). **Litigation,** the act of engaging in a civil lawsuit, has become more common in recent years.

As explained in the chapter introduction, if your company is sued, you as a RIM professional may be asked to locate and organize documents containing facts related to issues in the lawsuit. You must also ensure that documents are destroyed

- Crime such as theft and sabotage
- Disasters such as floods, leaks, fires, and storms
- Civil litigation against the company
- Legal action by government for noncompliance with laws and regulations

only as part of a planned, approved program. You must also be aware of litigation pending against your company so that you refrain from destroying any records that might be relevant to the case, even if destruction has otherwise been approved. Finally, as a custodian of records, you should become familiar with the rules in your state regarding the **admissibility into evidence** of business documents and records. The RIM employee should be aware of court rules that govern the admissibility into evidence of an original document and/or a photocopy, microfilm copy, or computer software copy of that document.

As with any other phase of business, records and information management involves risks. The risks can be minimized by spending the money necessary to control them. Prudent managers will weigh the costs against the benefits of reducing risk before implementing a records and information management program. Risks that the RIM professional must be aware of are listed below.

Ethical Issues

Matters of business ethics are especially relevant to the records and information management professional. Violations of good business ethics frequently bring about criminal and civil legal disputes. The disputes, in turn, often require that records be produced to document activities.

Table 3.1 shows a few examples of ethical business management behaviors and their likely consequences.

Table 3.2 shows examples of unethical business management behaviors and their likely consequences.

The adoption of ethical policies by the owners and managers of a business is in the best interest of the business, its

Table 3.1: Ethical Business Management	
Ethical Behavior	**Likely Consequence**
Honest pricing	Customer trust and loyalty
Fair pay and benefits for employees	Employee productivity and loyalty
Straightforward advertising	Increased sales
Manufacture of safe products	Decreased liability; increased customer trust

Table 3.2: Unethical Business Management	
Unethical Behavior	**Likely Consequence**
Price fixing	Criminal action; loss of good reputation
Low pay, poor benefits for employees	Low productivity and morale
False or misleading advertising	Reduced sales; customer dissatisfaction
Intentional skimping on product quality and safety	Lawsuits; returned goods; loss of repeat business

employees, and its customers. Thus, it is also the responsibility of the records and information manager to follow policies of high ethical standards.

Such policies include maintaining the confidentiality of records, ensuring high-quality service in the management of information, and reporting honestly to management and regulatory agencies on the activities of the records units within the organization.

Finally, records and information managers must set high standards of ethical business behavior for any employees under their supervision.

Your Understanding

What are some risks faced by a RIM professional?

TERMS TO KNOW

▼

1. Review these key terms and important terms.

- **admissibility into evidence**
- **civil law**
- **copyright**

- **criminal law**
- **litigation**
- **software piracy**

2. Use each of the key terms in a sentence. Underline or italicize each term.

DISCUSSION QUESTIONS

▼

Answer each question as a written assignment or for class discussion. Be concise in your responses.

1. What is the difference between criminal law and civil law?

2. What are three classifications of government laws and regulations?

3. What is an important source of information for the government when it must determine whether or not a business is abiding by applicable laws and regulations?

4. What is the intent of the Paperwork Reduction Act of 1980?

5. What two rights are guaranteed to citizens by the Freedom of Information Act?

6. What federal law denies access to one's personal records without that person's permission?

7. As a RIM professional, what are two ways in which you should comply with copyright laws?

8. Why has it become more important in recent years for the RIM employee to be aware of civil legal matters?

9. How should the RIM professional deal with the possibility of litigation against the company?

10. Explain why ethical business management is in the best interest of the organization.

11. Name two or more policies that the records and information manager might adopt to ensure high ethical standards.

CRITICAL THINKING
▼

1. **Gather Facts**   Interview an administrator at your school or college to determine what legal guidelines related to student records are followed. Summarize the information in a written report.

2. **Generalize from Facts**   Make a general statement about the extent you believe the identified guidelines provide adequate protection to you, the student.

   Write a second statement about the extent you believe the identified guidelines are in the best interests of the school or college.

3. **Create New Ideas**   Develop a draft statement titled Guidelines for Student Records at [name of your school or college].

   Discuss your guidelines with those of other students and make revisions, if appropriate.

NETWORKING WITH THE REAL WORLD
▼

Use the Internet to research the topic "The legal perils of e-mail." Report your findings orally or in writing.

IMPLEMENTING UNIT 1 CONCEPTS

▼

GROUP ACTIVITY

Study the information system of a business in your community. Questions that might be investigated in your study are:

1. What are the primary information needs of the business?

2. Who decides what information is to be kept?

3. What are the job title and specific duties of the person in charge of records and information management?

4. Where does this person fit into the hierarchy of the business?

5. How does the business deal with each of the seven functions of RIM?

INDIVIDUAL INQUIRY

Interview one of the following: a RIM professional, a businessperson who deals with RIM but has another specialty, a government employee who works closely with records and information, or a librarian or library assistant. Write your own list of questions before you conduct the interview. Examples are:

1. What professional training have you had?

2. What RIM experience do you have?

3. Are you a member of a RIM professional association?

4. Do you enjoy working in the field of RIM?

5. Has your organization ever been involved in litigation in which records were an important element? (Ethical practice may prevent the employee from answering this question.)

6. Does your organization have policies concerning ethical professional conduct?

7. What records and information do you keep to comply with government laws or regulations?

SYNTHESIZING UNIT 1 CONCEPTS
▼

GROUP ACTIVITY

The members of your group have established a new business called *Professional RIM Consultants*. You have decided that before you begin to advertise your services, you will develop a statement of purpose, including a statement of ethical business practices and RIM behavior.

- Develop such a statement in approximately two double-spaced pages.

- Have other members of your class evaluate the statement.

- Make revisions if you think they are warranted.

Note: Your statement of purpose might give attention to such matters as:

- Compensation for the business owner

- Pricing

- Pay and benefits

- Advertising

- Safety of manufactured products

- Confidentiality

INDIVIDUAL INQUIRY

As a records and information management professional, you have been asked by your employer to destroy the file of design documents related to one of your company's products. You know that customers have taken legal action against your company because the product in question is considered unsafe. Describe how you will respond to this difficult situation.

Note: Consider the likely consequences of unethical business practices listed in Table 3.2 on page 27.

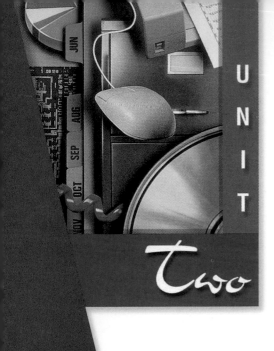

Managing

Nonelectronic

Records

In Unit 2 you will learn how to handle

the mountains of paperwork that enter

and leave organizations every working day.

This unit considers two major questions:

(1) How are incoming paper records

(also known as hard copy mail) received,

screened, documented, and managed?

(2) What procedures should be followed

when creating internal and outgoing paper-

work? You will also learn how important

paper records are stored in organized files

and how they are safeguarded, retrieved,

controlled, and destroyed.

PROFESSIONAL PROFILE

ELIZABETH CURTIS
Columbus, Ohio

Meet Elizabeth Curtis. Elizabeth is Director, Medical Information Management, at The Ohio State University's Medical Center in Columbus, Ohio. In this capacity, Elizabeth manages a staff of 85 employees in four hospital locations and seven medical information management offices. She directs this staff in performing and managing the collection of data and in maintaining, releasing, and analyzing both electronic and paper-based medical records.

Elizabeth's Career Path. Elizabeth has been with The Ohio State University for 17 years—13 years in her current position and 4 years as Associate Director, Medical Information Management. For two years prior to that she was an Assistant Director of Medical Records at Children's Medical Center in Dayton, Ohio. Elizabeth has a Bachelor of Science degree in Allied Health Professions.

Receipt and Creation of Hard Copy Records

The purpose of Chapter 4 is to enable you to:

- Recognize the overabundance of paperwork.
- Differentiate between paperwork and paper records.
- Enumerate questions to be answered when dealing with paperwork.
- Identify the different types and sources of incoming paperwork.
- Recall the procedures for opening hard-copy mail.
- Differentiate among voice mail, e-mail, and fax documents.
- Recognize the costs of keeping versus discarding paperwork.
- Provide examples of paperwork to be kept and paperwork to be discarded.
- Identify the different types and sources of outgoing and internal paperwork.
- Explain how the creation of paperwork can be minimized.
- Indicate how to manage the use of copying machines.
- Detail general principles to be followed in the design of business forms.
- Identify forms design and form filling software.

KEY TERMS

- business forms
- e-mail
- fax
- form filling software
- forms design software
- hard copy mail
- incoming paperwork
- internal paperwork
- outgoing paperwork
- voice mail

One of the most difficult jobs of the records and information professional is dealing with the profusion of paperwork that is typical of most offices. Just a few decades ago advances in office technology prompted the prediction of "paperless offices," but those advances have had just the opposite effect. Technological developments such as copying machines, plain-paper fax machines, laser and inkjet printers, high-speed departmental computer printers, and less expensive offset printing equipment have all made it easier and more tempting to produce paperwork. Numerous local, state, and federal government regulations require more recordkeeping each year. Many of these records are stored on paper. In spite of the fact that organizations keep much of their data on computers and other nonpaper media, they still have more paperwork than ever to handle.

Where Does All the Paperwork Come From?	
Incoming Paper	Outgoing and Internal Paper
United States Postal Service (USPS) mail	Copies of USPS mail sent
Fax messages	Originals of fax messages
Parcel delivery service	Copies of items delivered
Messenger, incoming	Messenger deliveries, internal
Written notes of voice messages	Internally generated reports
E-mail printouts	Internal memorandums

Not Every Piece of Paper Is a Record

The major error in handling paperwork is to assume that every piece of paper is a record worth keeping. To be classified as a record, a piece of paper must have value to the organization, and it must be more costly for the organization to throw it away than to keep it. Most paper items do not meet these requirements. Much incoming paperwork is often called "junk

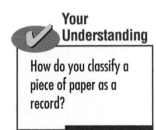

Your Understanding

How do you classify a piece of paper as a record?

mail," and it should be kept only temporarily or discarded immediately. The records and information professional must recognize the difference between paperwork that is of no value to the organization (and is discarded) and paperwork that *is* of value (and is kept as a record to be managed).

The Paperwork Dilemma

The records professional must determine the answers to several difficult questions when dealing with the excessive paperwork found in business today:

1. What are the sources and types of paperwork?
2. What are the costs of keeping versus discarding paperwork?
3. Which incoming paperwork items are records to be kept and which should be discarded?
4. Of the records that are kept, which should be converted to micrographic or electronic form and which should be retained on paper?
5. How and where should paper records be stored so they can be retrieved?
6. How can the organization minimize the creation, and therefore the cost, of internal and outgoing paperwork?

Let's consider the answer to the first question: What are the sources and types of paperwork? Paperwork that comes into the organization from outside sources is called incoming. Paperwork generated within the organization is called internal and outgoing.

Sources of incoming mail

- Incoming paper mail
- Fax
- Voice mail
- E-mail

Incoming Paperwork

Incoming paperwork arrives from sources outside the organization. Any kind of mail that arrives on paper is called **hard copy mail.** Although much incoming paperwork still arrives via the U.S. Postal Service, other sources include parcel delivery services, messenger services, and incoming written telephone messages. Another type of incoming paperwork is received by fax machine. A **fax** is a copy of a document sent from one facsimile machine to another over telephone lines

(see **Figure 4.1**). **Voice mail** is a recorded message that is transmitted from one telephone to another. It is not in paper form until someone actually writes the message. **E-mail,** or electronic mail, is a message or other document sent from one computer to one or more other computers. Paperwork for e-mail is created only if the incoming e-mail is printed. How incoming paperwork is received, screened, documented, and managed depends on the volume of paper received and the size and type of organization. For example, in large organizations, mail can be sorted and even opened by machine. In smaller organizations where incoming hard-copy mail takes many forms, it may be wise to adopt the steps listed below when opening mail.

Your Understanding

What are some sources of hard copy mail?

How to Open the Mail

1. **Prioritize.** With a trash can or recycling bin within reach, separate third-class or bulk mail from first-class mail. Look at, or screen, the mail and decide whether to discard third-class mail prior to opening. Follow steps 2 through 5 for each item before going to the next piece of mail.
2. **Open.** Open first-class mail first.
3. **Classify.** Screen again and classify first-class items as records that should be kept or paperwork that should be discarded.

4. **Organize.** Discard the envelope if the return address is inside. Unfold heavily creased items so they will lie flat. Put multiple pages and enclosures in a logical order. Staple multiple pages diagonally in the upper left corner. Avoid the use of paper clips except for enclosures to be processed separately. Decide if enclosures, such as checks, are to be separated for special processing.

5. **Document.** Consider whether or not to stamp the time and date of receipt on the item. Consider whether to place a routing notation on the item.

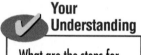

Your Understanding

What are the steps for opening mail?

Costs of Keeping Versus Discarding Paperwork

The successful records and information professional is always aware of how much it costs to keep paperwork compared with how much keeping the paperwork is worth to the organization. With some exceptions, the RIM professional will say, "If it costs more to keep than the record is worth, throw it away!" For example, the following chart shows in the left column some of the costs associated with *keeping* paperwork;

Costs of Keeping Paperwork	Costs of Discarding Paperwork
File cabinets; other file equipment	Lack of documentation when needed
Filing supplies such as folders	Document recovery cost
Labor of file workers	Recycling or disposal cost
Rent or capital cost of floor space	Government penalties for incomplete records
Overhead, such as heat, light, etc.	
Litigation losses because records that could have been destroyed legally were kept and presented in court, and the facts contained therein proved unfavorable	Lack of historical information
	Litigation losses because records favorable to litigation are missing
Crowded files making important records hard to find	Lack of information for research needs

the right column lists costs that might be incurred if needed paperwork is discarded.

It is not easy to figure the exact dollar costs of most of the items in the above chart. As records and information professionals gain experience, however, they will be able to make intelligent decisions about what to keep—and for how long. Much incoming paperwork can safely be discarded close to the time it is received. Examples of incoming paperwork that should become part of the records of an organization and paperwork that probably should be discarded are listed in the following chart.

Incoming Paperwork: Examples of What to Keep and What to Discard	
Keep	Discard
Correspondence requiring a response	Correspondence not requiring action
Financial and accounting records	Notices and announcements when no action is required
Legal documents such as contracts, deeds, notes, and agreements	Advertisements for products and services not needed
Employee records	Any information that is already available

Outgoing and Internal Paperwork

Outgoing paperwork includes the copies company keeps of documents that are sent outside the organization, such as a copy you might keep of a letter sent to another company. It is not necessary to keep a paper record of everything sent out. For example, a copy of a letter saved on a computer disk may be a satisfactory replacement for a paper copy. In many cases, it is not even necessary to keep the disk record. An example is a routine acknowledgment of an order that has already been entered into the sales system of the company.

Outgoing paperwork also includes the originals that are faxed to others and copies of documents delivered by parcel delivery and messenger.

- Follow cost-controlling guidelines for equipment
- Recycle wastepaper
- Use form-filling computer software
- Carefully manage design of forms

Internal paperwork is a means of communication within an organization and is distributed by fax or messenger from one office of the organization to another. It includes internally generated reports, internal memorandums, and any information on paper that stays within the organization. Examples include work schedules, pay notices to employees, internal company newsletters, company policies and procedures, and requests for information. Internal communication is being replaced more and more by voice mail and e-mail.

Minimizing the Creation of Paperwork

The records and information professional is responsible for giving careful thought to the creation of paperwork. The basic principles to be followed are:

1. Create a record only if it serves the organization and its clients or customers.

2. Consider alternatives to paper records such as computer records and e-mail.

3. If a paper record must be created, use the most efficient and effective means possible.
   - Follow carefully cost-controlling guidelines for the use of any equipment that produces paper records.
   - Adopt procedures for recycling wastepaper to help protect the environment.
   - Consider the use of form filling computer software to make filling in forms more efficient.
   - Design paper forms so they can be completed easily and accurately.

4. Use paper efficiently when creating a record.
   - When creating multiple copies of any paper record, create only the number needed.
   - Avoid the use of paper that is not a standard size; avoid the use of legal-size paper and legal-size filing cabinets.
   - Adopt policies concerning the desired length of reports, memorandums, and other documents. For example, some companies have a policy of keeping internal memos to a maximum length of one page.

- Control the number of copies made
- Use standard-size paper
- Limit length of documents
- Print single-spaced and on both sides of the paper

- Consider single-spacing reports and other materials and using both sides of the paper. This practice not only saves paper but also makes filing easier.

Your Understanding

What are the basic principles of creating paper records?

Copy Machine Management

There is a close relationship between mismanagement and misuse of office copying equipment and excess paperwork. The guidelines below can save time and money by eliminating unnecessary duplication of paper records. An amusing example of how difficult it may be to rid the office of unnecessary paperwork appeared in the 1992 United States Post Office publication *1942: Into the Battle*: "A bureaucrat . . . persisted in getting the eleven endorsements needed to destroy some redundant files, and final approval was at last obtained—with the proviso that he first make one copy of everything destroyed."

Guidelines for Managing Copying Machines

- Allow employees to make only business-related copies.
- Keep track of who uses the copier and the number of copies made.
- Make copiers accessible to employees who need them for business use.
- Consider the possibility of employing copying machine operators.
- Send large-volume copying jobs to a reproduction center or commercial printing company.
- Establish employee training programs on the economical use of copying machines and how to avoid waste.

Business Forms Management

Business forms, which are paper records that have blank spaces to be filled in, must be designed carefully for efficient use. Examples of business forms are employee applications,

Figure 4.2

Business Forms

```
                              ORDER FORM

     NAME _____ ADDRESS _____
     CITY _____ STATE _____ ZIP _____
     PHONE ( ) _____ NUMBER OF TITLES REQUESTED _____
     DATE NEEDED _____

     Title No. 1 _____ Author(s) _____
     ISBN (on back cover)_____ No. of Copies _____

     Title No. 2 _____ Author(s) _____
     ISBN (on back cover)_____ No. of Copies _____

     Title No. 3 _____ Author(s) _____
     ISBN (on back cover)_____ No. of Copies _____

     Title No. 4 _____ Author(s) _____
     ISBN (on back cover)_____ No. of Copies _____

     Title No. 5 _____ Author(s) _____
     ISBN (on back cover)_____ No. of Copies _____

     All items will be shipped and billed to the above address.
```

(a) A poorly designed business form.

```
                              ORDER FORM

     NAME _____
                Last            First          Middle Initial

     STREET ADDRESS _____

     CITY _____

     STATE _____ ZIP _____

     PHONE  Work: (  )          ext.:      Home: (  ) _____

     NUMBER OF TITLES REQUESTD _____ DATE NEEDED ____
            (5 title limit)

     Title No. 1 _____

     Author(s) _____

     ISBN (on back cover)_____ No. of Copies _____

     Title No. 2 _____

     Author(s) _____

     ISBN (on back cover)_____ No. of Copies _____

     Title No. 3 _____

     Author(s) _____

     ISBN (on back cover)_____ No. of Copies _____

     Title No. 4 _____

     Author(s) _____

     ISBN (on back cover)____   _____ No. of Copies _____

     Title No. 5 _____

     Author(s) _____

     ISBN (on back cover)_____ No. of Copies _____

     All items will be shipped and billed to the above address.
```

(b) A well designed business form. *What features make this a well designed form?*

invoices, sales slips, receipts, and applications for credit. Records and information professionals are often in charge of designing forms used in the organization. By observing important guidelines for designing business forms, the RIM professional can make the task of handling paperwork easier and less costly for the organization. **Figure 4.2** on page 42 shows examples of well-designed and poorly designed business forms.

Guidelines for Designing Business Forms

- Use standard-size paper.
- Arrange information in a logical order.
- Use distinctive captions.
- Place detailed instructions on the back of the form.
- Provide adequate space for requested information.
- Horizontal spacing should accommodate responses whether they are written or keyed; vertical spacing should be the standard vertical spacing of a computer printer or typewriter.
- Use color or other designation to indicate the use of each copy.

Forms-Design and Form-Filling Software

Computer software that can be used both to design forms and to fill in blank forms is available. **Forms design software** is a computer program that helps employees design efficient business forms at the computer. Efficient business forms comply with guidelines similar to those listed in the box. The software helps the designer to lay out the form neatly and logically to make changes easily, without starting over.

Form filling software is a computer program that enables employees to fill in business forms using a computer printer instead of a typewriter. A blank form is placed in the tray of the computer printer, and the blanks in the form are printed with data that have been keyed into the computer keyboard.

TERMS TO KNOW

▼

1. Review these key terms and important terms.

- **business forms**
- **e-mail**
- **fax**
- **form filling software**
- **forms design software**
- **hard copy mail**
- **incoming paperwork**
- **internal paperwork**
- **outgoing paperwork**
- **voice mail**

2. Assume that each key term is the answer to a question. Write a question for each answer.

DISCUSSION QUESTIONS

▼

Answer each question as a written assignment or for class discussion. Be concise in your responses.

1. Why do organizations have increasing amounts of paperwork to handle?
2. What is hard copy mail?
3. What is the first step in opening the mail in a small organization?
4. How does knowing the cost of keeping paperwork help you to decide whether or not to keep it?
5. Is it always necessary to keep a hard copy of paperwork that is sent out of the organization? If not, what is one alternative to saving a hard copy?
6. Give three examples of internal paperwork.
7. Name two alternatives to creating paper records.
8. Name two ways to save paper when creating records.
9. Where should detailed instructions appear on a business form?
10. How might the use of form-filling software be more efficient than filling out forms with a typewriter?

CRITICAL THINKING

1. **Gather Facts**   Conduct an inventory of your personal paperwork habits. Prepare a report that describes how you open the mail and handle e-mail; what you do with important papers; how often you lose needed paperwork; how you decide to dispose of paperwork; and any problems that you have related to paperwork at home, on the job, and/or at school.

2. **Generalize from Facts**   Prioritize and list changes in your personal paperwork habits that you believe will streamline your daily paperwork challenges. Your list should be in order from most important change to least important change.

3. **Create New Ideas**   Create a personal paperwork management plan for yourself that addresses the changes identified above. Prepare a written report that details your plan and is specific about where and under what headings important papers are to be filed.

NETWORKING WITH THE REAL WORLD

Access *Create Your Future.* The address is http://www.career-planning.com. Using this resource as a guide, write a one- to two-page career plan for yourself.

CHAPTER 5

Indexing and Alphabetizing Procedures

The purpose of Chapter 5 is to enable you to:

- Define *unit, indexing, alphabetizing,* and *case.*
- Index and alphabetize names of individuals.
- Index and alphabetize organization names.
- Index and alphabetize government names.
- Index and alphabetize addresses.
- Cross-reference names when appropriate.

KEY TERMS

- **alphabetic filing**
- **alphabetizing**
- **case**
- **cross-reference**
- **indexing**
- **lowercase**
- **unit**
- **uppercase**

Every record must be identified so that it can be located when needed. Records are often identified by an individual's name or a company's name appearing on the record. Organizing records according to the sequence of letters in the alphabet is called **alphabetic filing**. To standardize the way in which records are filed alphabetically, ARMA International has published rules for alphabetic filing. The twelve rules you will learn in this chapter follow the same principles as the ARMA rules.

Terms Related to the Filing Rules

Before studying the twelve filing rules, you must first understand four terms used in alphabetic filing.

Unit

Each part of a name is a **unit**. The name *Tasha Jamar Clendennin* has three units: *Tasha, Jamar,* and *Clendennin.* The name *Millennium Internet Merchandising Company* has four units. *The New Hampshire Camping Club* has five units.

Indexing

Indexing is determining the order and format of the units in a name when alphabetizing. To index names, we must know the answer to several questions. Is a person's record filed by first name or by last name? Is a business record filed under *T* if the name begins with *The?* Is punctuation considered in alphabetizing a name? You will learn the answers to these and other questions about indexing as you study the twelve filing rules.

Alphabetizing

When you arrange names in alphabetic order, you are **alphabetizing** them. The names *Elkins, Fong,* and *Guevara* are arranged in alphabetic order because *E* comes before *F,* and *F* comes before *G.* The names *Vaughan, Ventner,* and *Viegas* are also arranged in alphabetic order. They each begin with *V,* but the second letter is different. These second letters are in correct alphabetic order: *a* comes before *e,* and *e* comes before *i.*

Case

The **case** of a letter refers to whether the letter is written as a capital letter (A), called **uppercase,** or written as a small letter (a), called **lowercase.** In alphabetizing, an uppercase letter is treated the same as a lowercase letter. For example, the name McKnight is considered to be exactly the same as Mcknight.

Filing Rule Terms

- Unit
- Indexing
- Alphabetizing
- Case

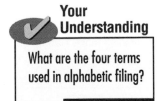

Your Understanding

What are the four terms used in alphabetic filing?

Alphabetizing Unit by Unit

Before you learn the filing rules, you must be able to alphabetize names unit by unit. In the following chart, the names are divided into units.

Name	Unit 1	Unit 2	Unit 3
Pastryshop	Pastryshop		
Pegasus Company	Pegasus	Company	
Pegasus Industries	Pegasus	Industries	
Rambo Computerworks	Rambo	Computerworks	
Rambo Deli Confections	Rambo	Deli	Confections
Rambo Deli Dining	Rambo	Deli	Dining

The first step in alphabetizing unit by unit is to alphabetize first units. Note the following about the above chart:

1. The names under Unit 1 are in alphabetic order.

2. The name *Pegasus* appears twice in the Unit 1 column. If first units are the same, the second step in alphabetizing unit by unit is to alphabetize second units. In the chart above, note that the names beside *Pegasus* under Unit 2, *Company* and *Industries,* are in alphabetic order.

3. The name *Rambo* appears three times in the Unit 1 column. If first *and* second units are the same, the next step in alphabetizing unit by unit is to alphabetize third units. In the chart above, note that the third units, *Confections* and *Dining,* determine the alphabetic order of the last two names.

Note

When alphabetizing, nothing comes before something.

Nothing Comes Before Something

In alphabetizing, an important guideline to remember is *nothing comes before something.* A name such as *Park* comes before a name such as *Parke*. Another example is shown in the chart below.

Name	Unit 1	Unit 2
Cyberchallenge	Cyberchallenge	
Cyberchallenge Games	Cyberchallenge	Games

Note that *Cyberchallenge* comes before *Cyberchallenge Games* because nothing comes before something *(Games)*.

A third example of the *nothing-comes-before-something* principle is shown below.

Name	Unit 1	Unit 2	Unit 3
Mitchell Pan Cookers	Mitchell	Pan	Cookers
Mitchell Pancake House	Mitchell	Pancake	House

In the example above, *Mitchell Pan Cookers* comes before *Mitchell Pancake House* because *Pan* comes before *Pancake*.

The Twelve Filing Rules

RULE 1: NAMES OF INDIVIDUALS. When indexing the name of a person, arrange the units in this order: last name as Unit 1, first name or initial as Unit 2, and middle name or initial as Unit 3. Periods are not used in indexing.

Name	Indexed Name
T. E. Ackerman	Ackerman T E
Jamal Rashad	Rashad Jamal
Jamal S. Rashad	Rashad Jamal S
C. Tyna Sanchez	Sanchez C Tyna
Carla Marie Sanchez	Sanchez Carla Marie

RULE 1: PRACTICE.   (1) Write or key each name in indexed order as in the example. Do not include the period after an initial. (2) Show the alphabetic order of the five names by writing *1* at the left of the first name, *2* at the left of the second, and so on. The example shows how a set of five names is indexed and alphabetized.

Example

D. R. Ross	_3_	Ross D R
Teresa D. Rawlings	_2_	Rawlings Teresa D
E. D. Smithwicke	_4_	Smithwicke E D
Ward H. Allison	_1_	Allison Ward H
Della Southern	_5_	Southern Della

Index and alphabetize the following names. Present your work in the same format as the example.

Jerry D. Moore

L. Teresa Valentino

Charles Lamb

Ross Will Valentine

Tony Lam

RULE 2: PERSONAL NAMES WITH PREFIXES.   Consider a prefix, such as *Mc* in *McDonald*, as part of the name it precedes. Ignore any apostrophe or space that appears within or after the prefix. Commonly used prefixes are *d', D', de, De, Del, De la, Di, Du, El, Fitz, La, Le, M, Mac, Mc, O', Saint, St., Van, Van de, Van der, Von,* and *Von der.*

Name	Indexed Name
Emma J. De Hart	DeHart Emma J
Charles Dean MacDowell	MacDowell Charles Dean
Phillip O'Day	ODay Phillip
Linda Saint John	SaintJohn Linda
Charlotte L. St.Jean	StJean Charlotte L
Ashley VanAllen	VanAllen Ashley
Jenah A. Van Balen	VanBalen Jenah A

RULE 2: PRACTICE. (1) Write or key each name in indexed order. (2) Show the alphabetic order of the five names by writing *1* at the left of the first name, *2* at the left of the second, and so on. Present your work in the same format as the example on page 50.

> Lisa S. O'Brien
>
> Frederick Von der Busch
>
> Richard O'Neal
>
> Gus Vonderahe
>
> Martin Oneal

RULE 3: HYPHENATED PERSONAL NAMES. Consider a hyphenated first, middle, or last name as one unit.

Name	Indexed Name
Willard G. Corvin-Rojas	CorvinRojas Willard G
Shawn-Lea Czinzack	Czinzack ShawnLea
Johanna Dejong	Dejong Johanna
Antonio R. Dejong-Valdez	DejongValdez Antonio R

RULE 3: PRACTICE. (1) Write or key each name in indexed order. (2) Show the alphabetic order of the five names by writing *1* at the left of the first name, *2* at the left of the second, and so on. Present your work in the same format as the example on page 50.

1 Lloyd Ray Harper-Huff

5 Lynette Wong

4 Lu-Lynn Wong

3 Luke Wong

2 Patrick Jones

RULE 4: ABBREVIATIONS OF PERSONAL NAMES. Abbreviated and shortened forms of personal names are not spelled out when indexed. For example, *Wm.* is indexed *Wm*, not *William*. *Liz* is indexed *Liz*, not *Elizabeth*.

Name	Indexed Name
Jos. R. Randolph	Randolph Jos R
Liz Ritchie	Ritchie Liz
Billy Dee Rowland	Rowland Billy Dee
Geo. Catlin Rutland	Rutland Geo Catlin

Filing Rules Related to Individuals

- Names of individuals
- Names with prefixes
- Hyphenated names
- Abbreviations of names
- Names with titles and suffixes

RULE 4: PRACTICE. (1) Write or key each name in indexed order. (2) Show the alphabetic order of the five names by writing *1* at the left of the first name, *2* at the left of the second, and so on. Present your work in the same format as the example on page 50.

Wm. G. Alvarez

Christine D'Agostino

Lou Kahn

Louis Kahn

Chas. D'Agostino

RULE 5: PERSONAL NAMES WITH TITLES AND SUFFIXES.

When appearing with a person's name, a title or a suffix is the last indexing unit used if it is needed to distinguish between two or more identical names. Titles and suffixes are indexed as written, except that periods are not used in indexing. Titles include *Capt., Dr., Mayor, Miss, Mr., Mrs., Ms.,* and *Senator.* Suffixes include seniority terms *(II, III, Jr., Sr.)* and professional designations *(CPA, CRM* [Certified Records Manager], *M.D., Ph.D.).*

Name	Indexed Name
Carol King, CPA	King Carol CPA
Dr. Carol King	King Carol Dr
Mrs. Holly W. Lazar	Lazar Holly W Mrs
Ms. Holly W. Lazar	Lazar Holly W Ms
Daryl E. Mabry, II	Mabry Daryl E II
Daryl E. Mabry, III	Mabry Daryl E III
Daryl E. Mabry, Jr.	Mabry Daryl E Jr
Daryl E. Mabry, Sr.	Mabry Daryl E Sr
Capt. Lisa R. Martino	Martino Lisa R Capt
Lisa R. Martino, CRM	Martino Lisa R CRM

Personal Name Considerations

- Names with prefixes
- Hyphenated names
- Abbreviated names
- Titles and suffixes
- Same names

RULE 5: PRACTICE. (1) Write or key each name in indexed order. (2) Show the alphabetic order of the five names by writing *1* at the left of the first name, *2* at the left of the second, and so on. Present your work in the same format as the example on page 50.

5. Dr. Ahmad R. Sahbie

1. Rev. James A. Lloyd

4. Linda Lopez-DeVilla, CPA

3. Linda Lopez-Devilla

2. James R. Lloyd

Your Understanding

How is an individual's name indexed?

RULE 6: NAMES OF BUSINESSES AND ORGANIZATIONS. Consider the units in business and organization names in the order in which they are normally written. When *The* is the first word of the name, it is indexed as the last unit. Names with prefixes are considered one unit, as with personal names.

Name	Indexed Name
Allegheny Realty	Allegheny Realty
Anna Lang Studios	Anna Lang Studios
The Bank of Vermont	Bank of Vermont The
C H Detective Agency*	C H Detective Agency
CH Detective Agency	CH Detective Agency
CJR Car Rentals	CJR Car Rentals
Dymock and Boucher	Dymock and Boucher
East Coast Fun Park	East Coast Fun Park
Eastcoasters Bicycles	Eastcoasters Bicycles
El Toro Industries	ElToro Industries
Hospital of Olympia	Hospital of Olympia
The Jackson Daily News	Jackson Daily News The
Marie Scott High School	Marie Scott High School
South East Laundromat	South East Laundromat
University of Utah	University of Utah

*C H Detective Agency comes before CH Detective Agency because nothing (a blank space) comes before something (in this case, the letter *H*).

RULE 6: PRACTICE. (1) Write or key each name in indexed order. (2) Show the alphabetic order of the five names by writing *1* at the left of the first name, *2* at the left of the second, and so on. Present your work in the same format as the example on page 50.

Parsell Furniture Company

Simmons and Conner

Master Locksmiths

Paul Simmons Corporation

Mister Submarine Cafe

RULE 7: ABBREVIATIONS IN BUSINESS AND ORGANIZATION NAMES. Abbreviations in business and organization names are not spelled out when indexed. For example, *Inc.* is indexed *Inc*, not *Incorporated*.

Name	Indexed Name
Carpets Ltd. of PA	Carpets Ltd of PA
Data Systems, Inc.	Data Systems Inc
Dr. Pepper Bottling Co.	Dr Pepper Bottling Co
Lt. Penn Equipment Co.	Lt Penn Equipment Co
Ms. Sport Smartwear	Ms Sport Smartwear
N. J. Boothe Agy.	N J Boothe Agy
Regal Mfg. Corp.	Regal Mfg Corp

RULE 7: PRACTICE. (1) Write or key each name in indexed order. (2) Show the alphabetic order of the five names by writing *1* at the left of the first name, *2* at the left of the second, and so on. Present your work in the same format as the example on page 50.

Micro Specialties, Inc.

Garden Supplies Co.

Farris Service Center, Inc.

Garza and Gravley, Attys.

Fashion Corner, Etc.

RULE 8: PUNCTUATION IN BUSINESS AND ORGANIZATION NAMES.

Ignore any punctuation marks that appear in business and organization names. As with personal names, hyphenated business and organization names are indexed as one unit. Punctuation marks include the apostrophe ('), colon (:), comma (,), dash (—), diagonal slash (/), exclamation point (!), hyphen (-), parentheses (), period (.), question mark (?), quotation marks (""), and semicolon (;).

Name	Indexed Name
"Bob" McFall Farms	Bob McFall Farms
Cole-Elliott Used Parts	ColeElliott Used Parts
Economy Rent-a-Car Co.	Economy RentaCar Co
For Joy! Tenniswear	For Joy Tenniswear
How's That? Burgers	Hows That Burgers

RULE 8: PRACTICE. (1) Write or key each name in indexed order. (2) Show the alphabetic order of the five names by writing *1* at the left of the first name, *2* at the left of the second, and so on. Present your work in the same format as the example on page 50.

Sara's Hot-Dogs, Inc.

"Sam" the Barber

Lil' Rascals Day Care

Sam's Fried Chicken

Lilly's Florist

RULE 9: NUMBERS IN BUSINESS AND ORGANIZATION NAMES.

Arabic numbers (*2, 17*) are considered one unit and are filed in numeric order before alphabetic characters. Hyphenated numbers (*7-11*) are indexed according to the number before the hyphen (*7*); the number after the hyphen (*11*) is ignored. An arabic number followed by a hyphen and a word (*7-Gable*) or a hyphen and a letter (*4-N-1*) is considered one unit (*7GABLE, 4N1*). Thus, names such as *7-11 Store, 4-N-1 Bargain Store, 6-20 Shop,* and *4-Seasons Restaurant* are indexed and alphabetized as *4N1 Bargain Store, 4Seasons Restaurant, 6 Shop,* and *7 Store.* If a number in a business or organization name is spelled out (*First* Street Pizza), it is filed alphabetically as written. Hyphenated numbers that are spelled out (*Twenty-One* Restaurant) are considered one unit (*TwentyOne* Restaurant). The letters *st, d,* and *th* following an arabic number are ignored. Thus *1st* is indexed as *1, 2nd* or *2d* as *2, 3rd* or *3d* as *3, 4th* as *4,* and so on.

Name	Indexed Name
7-11 Family Store	7 Family Store
7 Flags Over Texas	7 Flags Over Texas
7th Swan Swimwear Co.	7 Swan Swimwear Co
11 Pipers Music Shop	11 Pipers Music Shop
99 Flavors Yogurt Parlor	99 Flavors Yogurt Parlor
1400 Allendale Apts.	1400 Allendale Apts
Fifty-Fifty Autocars	FiftyFifty Autocars
Forty Mile Steakhouse	Forty Mile Steakhouse
Four Corners Pharmacy	Four Corners Pharmacy
Fourth and Main Photo	Fourth and Main Photo
Galen's 6-Way Wrench Co.	Galens 6Way Wrench Co
Galen's Auction Market	Galens Auction Market
Wayco 8 Way Carwash	Wayco 8 Way Carwash
The Wayco Eight, Inc.	Wayco Eight Inc The

RULE 9: PRACTICE. (1) Write or key each name in indexed order. (2) Show the alphabetic order of the five names by writing *1* at the left of the first name, *2* at the left of the second, and so on. Present your work in the same format as the example on page 50.

4 Mockingbirds Cafe

First Impressions Hairstyles

4 Columns Inn

1st Choice Auto Auction

One Lakeland Villa

RULE 10: SYMBOLS IN BUSINESS AND ORGANIZATION NAMES.
If a symbol is part of a name, the symbol is indexed as if it were spelled out, as shown here:

Symbol	Indexed As
&	and
¢	cent or cents
$	dollar or dollars
#	number, pound, or pounds
%	percent

Name	Indexed Name
1 # Hamburger Shop	1 Pound Hamburger Shop
58th Street Deli Mart	58 Street Deli Mart
The 58¢ Beef Giant	58cent Beef Giant The
A & R Appliances	A and R Appliances
$ Saver Used Appliances	Dollar Saver Used Appliances
# One Cellular Phones	Number One Cellular Phones
#1 Amusements	Number1 Amusements

RULE 10: PRACTICE. (1) Write or key each name in indexed order. (2) Show the alphabetic order of the five names by writing *1* at the left of the first name, *2* at the left of the second, and so on. Present your work in the same format as the example on page 50.

The Rogers & Kirk Co.

Nunez & Kelly

High $ Real Estate Agcy.

1 Motor Sales

M & M Food Store

Your
Understanding

How are business
names indexed?

RULE 11: STATE AND LOCAL GOVERNMENT NAMES. State and local government names are indexed first by the name of the state, county, or city that has immediate jurisdiction over that governmental agency. Therefore, to index state and local government names properly, you have to know if that agency, board, bureau, or department comes under the state, the county, the township, or the city. The function of the agency is considered next. Examples of functions are agriculture, commerce, defense, education, health, natural resources, planning, police, recreation, transportation, and welfare. Considered next in indexing government names is the designation of the office. Examples of the designation of an office are agency, board, bureau, commission, department, division, ministry, office, and service. If you have trouble recognizing or indexing government names, refer to the Blue Pages of a telephone directory, if they are available. The Blue Pages contain listings for local, county, state, and United States government names.

Name	Indexed Name

Board of Education
City of Freeport, ME
	Freeport City of
	    Education Board of
	    Freeport Maine

Bureau of Weights and Measures
State of Maine
Augusta, ME
	Maine State of
	    Weights and Measures Bureau of
	    Augusta Maine

RULE 11: PRACTICE (STATE AND LOCAL GOVERNMENT NAMES).

(1) Write or key each name in indexed order. (2) Show the alphabetic order of the three names by writing *1* at the left of the first name, *2* at the left of the second, and *3* at the left of the third. Present your work in the same format as the example on page 50.

Department of Social Services
City of Sheridan, Wyoming

Perry City Personnel Department
Perry, Missouri

Perry County Medical Examiner
Hazard, Kentucky

RULE 11 (CONTINUED): UNITED STATES GOVERNMENT NAMES.

United States government names are indexed first under *United States Government,* then by the function, followed by the designation of the office. In each of the following examples of U.S. government names, Unit 1 is *United,* Unit 2 is *States,* and Unit 3 is *Government.*

Name	Indexed Name
U.S. Department of Agriculture Forest Service	United States Government Agriculture Department of Forest Service
U.S. Treasury Department Customs Service	United States Government Treasury Department Customs Service

RULE 11: PRACTICE (UNITED STATES GOVERNMENT NAMES).

(1) Write or key each name in indexed order. (2) Show the alphabetic order of the three names by writing *1* at the left of the first name, *2* at the left of the second, and *3* at the left of the third. Present your work in the same format as the example on page 50.

U.S. Interior Department
National Park Service

U.S. Commerce Department
Census Bureau

U.S. Treasury Department
Bureau of Engraving & Printing

RULE 11 (CONTINUED): FOREIGN GOVERNMENT NAMES. Foreign government names are indexed first by the name of the country, then by the function of the governmental unit, and then by the designation of the office.

Name	Indexed Name
Ministry of Agriculture Tunisia	Tunisia Agriculture Ministry of
Department of Human Resources Venezuela	Venezuela Human Resources Department of

RULE 11: PRACTICE (FOREIGN GOVERNMENT NAMES).
(1) Write or key each name in indexed order. (2) Show the alphabetic order of the three names by writing *1* at the left of the first name, *2* at the left of the second, and *3* at the left of the third. Present your work in the same format as the example on page 50.

Department of State
Australia

Consulate General
Germany

Industrial Development Authority
Peru

Your Understanding

How are government names indexed?

RULE 12: ADDRESSES. When names are otherwise identical, they may be filed by address. The elements of the address are considered in the following order: city, state (spelled in full), street name, quadrant (NE, NW, SE, SW), and house or building number.

Name	Indexed Name
Taco-House 6th Street Dallas, TX	TacoHouse Dallas Texas 6 Street
Taco-House 32 Grantham Avenue Dallas, TX	TacoHouse Dallas Texas Grantham Avenue 32
Taco-House 21840 Grantham Avenue Dallas, TX	TacoHouse Dallas Texas Grantham Avenue 21840
Taco-House 193 Hillary Street Dallas, TX	TacoHouse Dallas Texas Hillary Street 193
Taco-House 600 Ward Street, NE Pierre, SD	TacoHouse Pierre South Dakota Ward Street NE 600
Taco-House 600 Ward Street, SE Pierre, SD	TacoHouse Pierre South Dakota Ward Street SE 600

RULE 12: PRACTICE. (1) Write or key each name in indexed order. (2) Show the alphabetic order of the four names by writing *1* at the left of the first name, *2* at the left of the second, and so on. Present your work in the same format as the example on page 50.

Videoworld
257 Oak Street
Toledo, OH

Videoworld
110 Norris Avenue
Toledo, OH

Videoworld
1400 Norris Avenue
Toledo, OH

Videoworld
37 Ardmore Drive
Union, MT

Note

Additional indexing and alphabetizing practice is provided in Appendix A.

Cross-Referencing

A **cross-reference** is a notation that a name or record is filed elsewhere. For example, if a person changed her name from *Tasha Bowen* to *Tasha Rashad*, you would file records under the new name, *Tasha Rashad*. For a reasonable period of time, however, you would make a notation of the name change in the file. This notation, called a cross-reference, would be filed under the name *Tasha Bowen* in case someone requested records under her former name. A cross-reference would also be prepared in the following situations:

1. When it is difficult to determine which of a person's names is the last name. A name such as Feng Hou might be filed under *Hou* and cross-referenced under *Feng*.

2. When a person or company goes by more than one name, such as *Southland Corporation* and *7-11 Stores*. File records under the most-used name and cross-reference under the others.

TERMS TO KNOW

▼

1. Review these key terms and important terms.

- **alphabetic filing**
- **alphabetizing**
- **case**
- **cross-reference**

- **indexing**
- **lowercase**
- **unit**
- **uppercase**

2. Select a term from the above list for each of these definitions.

- Determining the order and format of the units in a name when alphabetizing.

- Arranging names in alphabetic order.

- Characters of the alphabet written as capital letters.

- Each part of a name that is considered separately when a name is indexed.

- Organizing records according to the sequence of letters in the alphabet.

- Characters of the alphabet written as small letters.

- A notation that a record is filed elsewhere.

- Refers to whether or not letters of the alphabet are capitalized.

DISCUSSION QUESTIONS

▼

Answer each question as a written assignment or for class discussion. Be concise in your responses.

1. Define *unit*.

2. Define *indexing*.

3. Define *alphabetizing*.

4. Define *case*.

CRITICAL THINKING

1. **Gather Facts**   Find the origin of the terms *uppercase* and *lowercase.*

2. **Generalize from Facts**   Write a general statement about why an uppercase letter is treated the same as a lowercase letter in alphabetizing.

3. **Create New Ideas**   Write a statement that addresses this question: "If an uppercase letter is treated the same as a lowercase letter, why not write everything in the same case and eliminate all the shifting?"

NETWORKING WITH THE REAL WORLD

Access the *Small Business Administration.* The address is http://www.sba.gov. Using this resource as a guide, list the major considerations to be addressed in starting a new business.

Systems for Organizing Paper Records

The purpose of Chapter 6 is to enable you to:

- Select equipment and supplies essential for the storage and maintenance of paper records.
- Follow efficient procedures for planning, establishing, and maintaining files for paper records.
- Identify the steps in alphabetic system entry and storage.
- Recognize alphabetic, subject, geographic, and numeric filing systems.

KEY TERMS

- chronological file
- cut
- ergonomics
- file folder
- file guide
- filing supplies
- geographic filing
- numeric filing
- storage equipment
- subject filing
- tab

Every record must be stored in some way so it can be protected, located, and retrieved when needed. Storing records requires not only **storage equipment** but also **filing supplies.** Storage equipment and filing supplies hold and identify records. File cabinets and folders hold the records; labels identify the contents within a cabinet and the contents within a folder. Proper storing and accurate labeling allow records to be easily located, identified, and retrieved—and easy retrieval is the main purpose of any filing system.

Equipment and Supplies for Paper Records

Storage equipment for paper records includes several types of file cabinets, sometimes called storage systems, and auxiliary equipment such as sorting devices and carts to move paper records to and from the files. File cabinets come in various types. The traditional four- or five-drawer file cabinet is still popular in many offices. Open-file shelves are also common because they store many records in a minimal amount of space and with easy access. Mobile systems, like the one shown in **Figure 6.1,** are popular when floor space is expensive or scarce.

Filing supplies include containers for paper records and accessories such as file dividers and labels. Several types of containers are available for paper records, the most popular of which are folders. There are many kinds of folders, but the two most popular are **file folders**, also known as manila folders, and hanging folders like those shown in **Figure 6.2**. File folders are made of heavy paper stock and come in different colors, the most common color being cream.

Storage Equipment

- File cabinets or storage systems
- Sorting devices
- Carts

Figure 6.1

An open-shelf, mobile system. *When do you think this type of system is best used?*

Figure 6.2

File folders and hanging folders. *How are hanging folders used differently than file folders?*

Hanging folders also come in an assortment of colors and have metal extensions that enable them to hang on file-drawer frames.

Note that the file folder has an extension at the top. This extension is called a **tab**; it is used to hold a label to identify the folder's contents. The width of the tab is referred to as its **cut**. If the tab is one-fifth as wide as the folder, it is called a one-fifth cut tab. If the tab is half as wide as the folder, it is a one-half cut tab. If the tab runs the full width of the folder, it is called a full-cut tab.

Other containers for paper records include file pockets (see **Figure 6.3**), notebooks, and computer printout binders (see **Figure 6.4**).

Another important filing supply item is the file divider, better known in business as a **file guide,** or guide. A guide is a cardboard sheet with a tab, as shown in **Figure 6.5**. It is used to support file folders and to label major sections of the file.

File labels are small, self-adhesive tags used to identify folders and guides **(Figure 6.6)**. Labels attach to the tab of a folder. The information on the label can be printed from data in the user's computer system.

Figure 6.3

File pockets. *Why might you use file pockets instead of file folders?*

Figure 6.4

Printout binders. *What are some advantages of printout binders over file folders?*

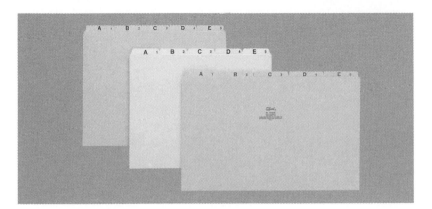

Figure 6.5

File guides. *How is a file guide different from a file folder?*

- Containers
- Folders
- File pockets
- Notebooks
- Computer printout binders
- File guides or dividers
- Labels

Figure 6.6

Computer-printed labels. File labels can be generated by a computer. *What are some advantages and disadvantages of using computer generated labels?*

Your Understanding

What are some common filing supplies?

File labels are also used to identify the contents of a file drawer. File drawer labels are inserted into the rectangular slot on the front of each file drawer.

Selecting Equipment and Supplies

Choosing the right equipment for paper records storage is an important responsibility of the records and information professional. Several factors must be considered when purchasing storage systems.

Room for Expansion

The amount of storage space should be adequate for both present and future records.

Fire Protection

Specially insulated file cabinets and other storage devices that afford varying degrees of fire protection are available. The cost of such equipment increases as the amount of fire protection increases. The extra cost of fire protection provided by the equipment should be weighed against the value of the records and how difficult they would be to replace.

Floor Space

The amount of floor space required by the equipment should be weighed against floor space costs, convenience of use, and the amount of space available for filing equipment. For example, if your company has a large amount of low-cost floor space, traditionally designed filing equipment might be the best investment. Conversely, if floor space in your organization is scarce, it might be wise to purchase special, space-saving equipment.

"Bells and Whistles"

The original purchase cost and subsequent maintenance costs of special equipment features, sometimes called "bells and whistles," should be weighed against the benefits of the special features. Two examples follow: (1) motorized files can be convenient to use, but they are also more expensive to purchase and repair than manually operated equipment; (2) locks for files should be purchased only if records in them are subject to security risks and only if company policy addresses procedures for issuing keys and using the locks.

Ergonomics

The equipment should be tailored to the overall ergonomic atmosphere of the office. **Ergonomics** is the applied science of conforming equipment, systems, and the working environment to the requirements of people, including those with disabilities.

Ergonomic factors to be considered in selecting equipment include design, color, acoustical treatment, security, safety, accessibility, and the relationship of the equipment to other office furnishings and accessories. The *Americans with Disabilities Act (ADA)*, a law that was passed in 1990, contains specific requirements related to accessibility to equipment by persons who have disabilities.

Standardized Equipment

If at all feasible, purchase standard-size equipment. Such equipment is likely to be usable in other offices and departments in case of reorganization. In addition, standard sizes are less expensive than irregular sizes. Professionals in RIM encourage standardization, as evidenced by a campaign sponsored by ARMA International. The campaign is called *ELF,* or

- Room for expansion
- Fire protection
- Floor space
- "Bells and whistles"
- Ergonomics
- Standardized equipment

Your Understanding

What are factors to be considered when purchasing storage systems?

"*Eliminate Legal Files*," and it urges organizations to stop using legal-size files and legal-size paper. A legal-size file cabinet is about three inches wider than a standard one. Legal-size paper, measuring $8\frac{1}{2}$ by 14 inches, is costly to handle and file compared with standard $8\frac{1}{2}$- by 11-inch paper.

Justifying Paper Files

Before paper files are established, the RIM professional is responsible for justifying their importance. Because paper files are both expensive and cumbersome, careful consideration should be given to the following questions:

1. Why must the records be retained on paper?

2. What sacrifices would be necessary if the paper records were converted to electronic or micrographic (tiny photographic) form?

3. What is the difference in cost between the paper-based system and a paperless system?

4. Have all of the extra costs been considered? For paper records systems, some of the costs include additional floor space, extra labor for handling records, and extra time for finding and retrieving paper records. For electronic and micrographic systems, extra costs include time and labor to convert paper to another format and the cost of special equipment needed to operate a paperless system.

Planning a Paper Records System

Once the decision has been made to establish a paper filing system, the RIM professional should plan the system carefully for maximum efficiency. Considerations in planning the system include:

1. **Volume of records:** What is the expected volume of records and on what time schedule will records be entered into the system?
2. **Location of records:** Will the files be centrally located and controlled or will they be located throughout the organization in areas where they are most likely to be used?
3. **Employee training:** What employee training is needed prior to implementing the system?
4. **Organization of files:** Should files be organized alphabetically, by subject, by geographic region, or numerically?
5. **Handling records:** What procedures will be followed in entering records into and retrieving records from the system?
6. **System operation:** Who will be responsible for the day-to-day operation of the system?

Planning Considerations

- Volume of records
- Location of recoreds
- Employee training
- Organization of files
- Handling records
- System operation

Alphabetic Filing Systems

As you learned in Chapter 5, records are frequently organized alphabetically according to the name of a person or organization. For example, a lawyer, physician, or dentist might arrange client or patient folders in alphabetic order. The guidance department in a school might arrange student folders alphabetically. The purchasing department of a retail store might have an alphabetic file containing a folder for each of its suppliers.

Important incoming correspondence and copies of important outgoing correspondence are kept and often arranged alphabetically, either in file folders or in a notebook. Some businesses keep a letter book, which is a notebook containing significant correspondence arranged in *chronological order,* that is, order by date.

Setting up a basic alphabetic system requires some type of file cabinet, file folders, and labels. Labels can be printed from a computer database or word processing system. If file drawers are used, each drawer should be identified with a label indicating

Your Understanding

What should be considered when planning a paper filing system?

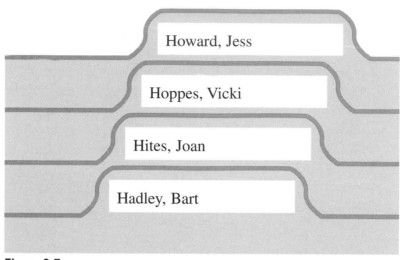

Figure 6.7

Aligning labels on folder tabs. ***What is one benefit of aligning labels?***

the range of its contents. Folder labels should be attached to the folder tabs so they align when folders are placed in the file. **Figure 6.7** shows the correct way to align labels on tabs.

Papers are stored inside file folders with the heading to the left and the front facing the user. To prevent loss, papers are sometimes attached to the inside of the folder with a metal or plastic binder. Most file folders can be expanded by creasing the scores along the bottom of the front flap, thus preventing papers from bulging out of the folder. In **Figure 6.8,** the lines at the bottom of the folder represent the expansion scores. When file guides are used, they should be labeled to indicate the range of records covered.

Figure 6.8

Standard file folder. Notice the scores along the bottom. ***What is the purpose of these scores?***

Alphabetic System Entry and Storage

After paper records have been screened and documented as described in Chapter 4, they are filed in an alphabetic system according to the following steps:

1. **System entry:** In this step, the record is examined to determine the name under which it is to be filed, the name is indexed according to the filing rules, and the indexed name is noted on the record. This notation can be a highlight, underscore, circling, or writing of the indexed name.

2. **Cross-reference:** In this step, the record is examined again to determine alternate captions, if any, by which the record might be searched. If alternate captions come to mind, a written notation, called a cross-reference, is prepared and placed in the file under the cross-reference caption as shown in **Figure 6.9**. The file under the cross-reference caption will contain only a card or sheet of paper indicating the main file. The employee will determine which caption will be the main file containing all of the records and which will be the cross-reference

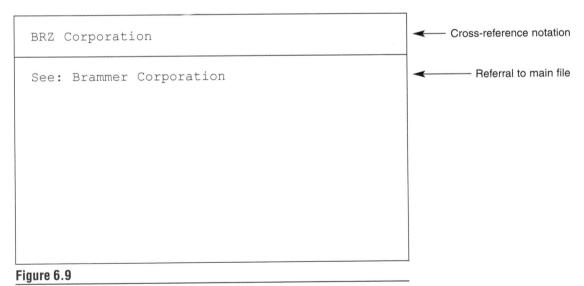

BRZ Corporation — Cross-reference notation

See: Brammer Corporation — Referral to main file

Figure 6.9

Cross-reference notation. *In what order would you fill out the cross-reference card and why?*

- System entry
- Cross-reference notation
- System storage
- Storage documentation

caption containing only the card or sheet of paper indicating the main file. An alternate cross-reference procedure involves copying the record and filing the copies under the alternate captions.

3. **System storage:** In this step, the record is alphabetized with others to be stored and then placed in the appropriate file container in the system.

4. **Storage documentation:** The final step is to document the fact that a group of records has been entered into the system and stored. A journal or log book as shown in **Figure 6.10** is used for this step, which is optional for small-scale systems.

DOCUMENTATION JOURNAL

Document Date	File Caption	Storage Date	Initials of Operator
3/15/--	ABC Corporation	3/30/--	AMD
3/16/--	Babbcock Limited	3/30/--	AMD
3/20/--	Anderson Supply	3/30/--	Cfg
4/1/--	Faxmore	4/19/--	Cfg

Figure 6.10

Documentation journal entries. *What is the importance of maintaining a documentation journal?*

Subject Filing Systems

It is often convenient to organize records according to topic or subject. For example, some records refer to products, processes, formulas, and other matters without containing the name of a person or organization. Such records are candidates for **subject filing.**

Sometimes it is helpful to group records according to topic even if they do contain names of individuals or organizations. For example, you might want to keep all your insurance policies in an *Insurance* folder rather than filing them under the name of the insurance company. A company might want to keep all its records about investments in one place rather than file them under the name of the investment broker or company. A folder captioned *Investments* can serve this purpose. The file shown in **Figure 6.11** combines alphabetic name captions with subject captions. This type of subject file is often found in smaller systems and desk-drawer files having few folders.

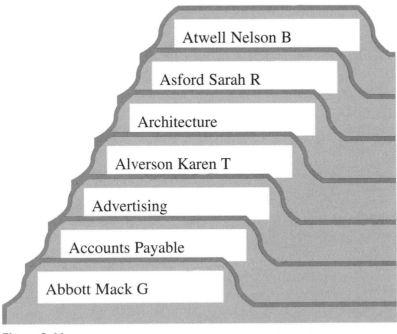

Figure 6.11

Combination subject file. *Which of these files are subject files?*

More elaborate subject files include the dictionary, encyclopedic, and subject-numeric types. In *dictionary subject files,* all of the captions are subjects, and the subjects are arranged in alphabetic order, as shown in **Figure 6.12.**

Encyclopedic subject files have alphabetized subject headings that are broken into subheadings. The subheadings are listed alphabetically under each main heading and may be followed by a general folder for each main heading. A *general caption* signals the location of an accumulation of records with varying subject captions. When an appropriate number of records containing the same subject caption accumulate, they will be refiled under their specific subject caption. For example, **Figure 6.13** shows a general folder labeled *Advertising General*. If five or more records related to Internet

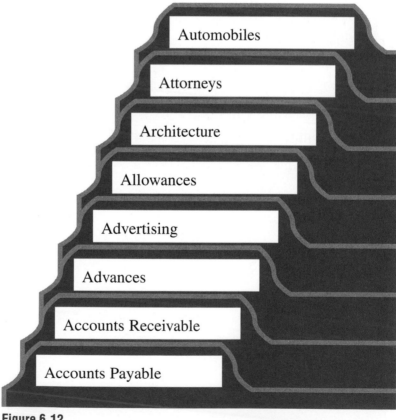

Figure 6.12

Dictionary subject file. *What is the difference between dictionary subject files and combination subject files?*

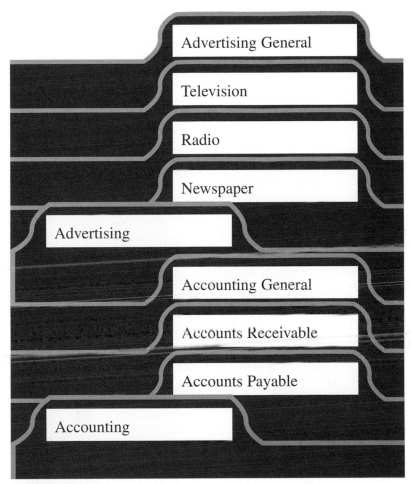

Figure 6.13

Encyclopedic subject file. *What is the difference between encyclopedic subject files and dictionary subject files?*

advertising were to accumulate in this general folder, a new folder would be prepared and labeled *Internet*. The Internet-related records would be removed from the general folder and stored in the *Internet* folder. Then the *Internet* folder would be placed in front of the *Newspaper* folder in the *Advertising* section of the file.

Subject-numeric files are similar to encyclopedic subject files except that numbers are used to identify the captions. For large systems, the use of numbers in subject files can make filing and locating records easier and quicker. See Figure 6.14 for an example of a subject-numeric file.

- Combination subject files
- Dictionary subject files
- Encyclopedic subject files
- Subject-numeric files

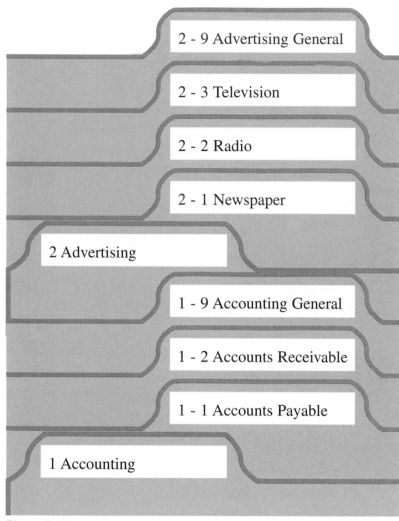

Figure 6.14

Subject-numeric file. *What advantages can you think of for using a subject-numeric file?*

Geographic Filing Systems

Some types of businesses file records according to geographic location, called a **geographic filing system,** as illustrated in **Figure 6.15.** For example, a sales business with definite geographic sales areas might organize certain records geographically by sales territory.

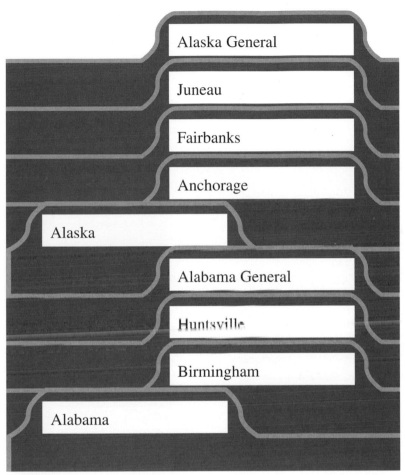

Figure 6.15

Geographic file. *What other file captions might you use instead of states and cities?*

Numeric Filing Systems

Many, if not most, business and organization records are filed by number. **Numeric filing systems** are easier to expand than alphabetic systems; new numbers can simply be added at the end of the file (see **Figure 6.16**). They are also more accurate for large files because the sequence of numbers is easier to recognize than the alphabetic sequence of names. Numeric systems are also unlikely to have duplicate captions, whereas duplicate names are quite frequent in large files.

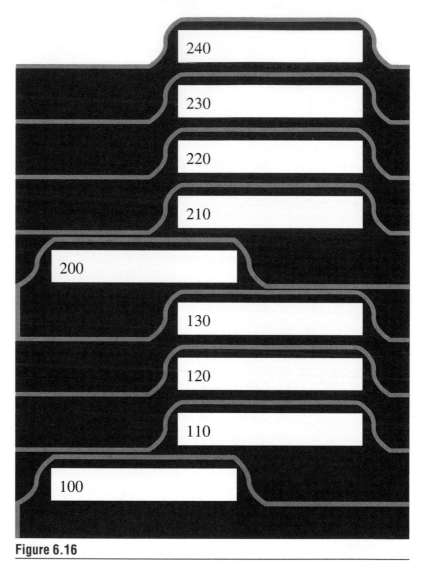

Figure 6.16

Numeric file. *How might you further subdivide this numeric system?*

Certain business records have preassigned numbers. Examples are forms such as sales invoices, purchase orders, receipts, shipping reports, and requisitions. These forms can be filed according to the preassigned numbers. One disadvantage of the numeric filing of such forms is that you must know the number of the form to find it in the files. This disadvantage can be eliminated by creating an alphabetic index to the file that lists, for example, vendor names in alphabetic order and related purchase order numbers for each vendor. However, it is still necessary to look in two places to find a record: the index and the numeric file. For this reason, numeric filing is frequently called an *indirect system.*

For other records, numbers must be assigned so that they can be filed numerically. Employee records, for example, might be arranged in the files numerically by an assigned employee number or an individual's social security number. Improved security is a major advantage of organizing employee records numerically. Anyone who is unfamiliar with the system will have difficulty locating a specific employee's file. However, even those who have authority to access employee files must frequently consult an index to find a specific employee number. Although this necessity is an extra, time-consuming step, it increases the confidentiality of the records by making them accessible only by indirect means.

Chronological Filing Systems

You have learned that chronological order means *order by date.* Documents to be acted on at a later date are often filed temporarily in a **chronological file**, where they are arranged in order according to the date they are to be acted on. For example, if a meeting must be attended on the afternoon of June 30, a notation of the meeting and perhaps a copy of the meeting agenda are filed under June 30. The user checks the file early each day to see if something has been filed under that day's date. A chronological file helps remove numerous unorganized papers from the desk until they are needed for action. This type of file also acts as a daily reminder that a certain report is due or that an important letter must be written. Other names for a chronological file are *tickler file* and *follow-up file.*

TERMS TO KNOW

▼

1. Review these key terms and important terms.
   - ADA
   - chronological file
   - chronological order
   - cross-reference
   - cut
   - dictionary subject files
   - ELF
   - encyclopedic subject files
   - ergonomics
   - file folder
   - file guide
   - file label
   - filing equipment
   - filing supplies
   - follow-up file
   - general caption
   - geographic filing
   - hanging folder
   - indirect system
   - numeric filing
   - storage equipment
   - subject filing
   - subject-numeric files
   - tab
   - tickler file

2. Write one or two paragraphs that contain each key term. Underline or italicize each term.

DISCUSSION QUESTIONS

▼

Answer each question as a written assignment or for class discussion. Be concise in your responses.

1. What are the purposes of a file guide?
2. What might be a disadvantage of purchasing motorized files rather than manually operated equipment?
3. What ergonomic factors should be considered when selecting records storage equipment?
4. What law was passed in 1990 that contains requirements related to accessibility to equipment?
5. Why has ARMA recommended that legal-size files and legal-size paper be eliminated from office use?
6. What are some of the extra costs associated with using paper records systems rather than paperless systems?

7. What are some of the extra costs associated with using electronic and micrographic systems?

8. In what order is correspondence arranged in a letter book?

9. In what direction should records be stored inside a file folder?

10. What is done in the system entry step of alphabetic system entry and storage?

11. What types of records are likely to be filed by subject?

12. What is the difference between dictionary and encyclopedic subject files?

13. What type of business might use geographic filing?

14. Name three advantages of numeric files over alphabetic files.

15. What is one disadvantage of numeric filing?

CRITICAL THINKING

1. **Gather Facts**   Visit an office supplies retailer or e-tailer. List the types of file cabinets available for sale and the cost of each.

2. **Generalize from Facts**   Which of the available file cabinets do you believe would be the best for your personal papers? What additional items would you purchase to develop your personal filing system? What is the total cost?

3. **Create New Ideas**   Write a statement that explains which filing system (alphabetic, subject, geographic, numeric, chronological) you would use for each of your records.

NETWORKING WITH THE REAL WORLD

Choose an item of office equipment that you would like to have. Access *Consumer Reports Online.* The address is http://www.ConsumerReports.org/. Using this resource as a guide, select a specific brand of the item of office equipment. Write a brief statement as to why you selected the brand.

Retrieval, Retention, and Recycling

> **The purpose of Chapter 7 is to enable you to:**
>
> - Describe procedures for retrieving records.
> - Recall legal requirements and procedures for retention.
> - Consider the advantages and disadvantages of alternate methods of records destruction.
> - Recognize the environmental benefits of recycling records.

KEY TERMS

- access
- delivery
- documentation
- follow-up
- out guide
- recovery
- recycle
- requisition
- retention
- retrieval

In this chapter, you will be introduced to retrieval, retention, and recycling—the three Rs of records and information management. Records that have been organized and stored in a filing system serve one purpose: use. However, it is possible to use records only if they are accessible. Thus, the function of **retrieval,** or obtaining filed records for use, is important to the RIM professional.

Records cannot be kept forever, so the RIM professional is also concerned with the amount of time that records are kept, or their **retention.** Finally, at the end of the retention period, the business discards the records.

When possible, paper records are **recycled** rather than simply thrown away. The recycled paper is then used in the manufacture of new paper and other products.

Retrieval

The function of records retrieval has five major components: access, documentation, delivery, follow-up, and recovery. These components are usually informal in small
organizations; in large organizations, each component may be
highly structured.

Access in a small paper filing system may simply entail
walking to a nearby file cabinet, scanning drawer labels, opening the drawer, scanning guide and folder tabs, locating a
folder, and removing either the entire folder or one or more
records from the folder. In a small company that uses computer files, access might simply mean clicking a mouse on one
or more screen icons.

In larger organizations, a **requisition,** a written request
for records, may have to be filled out and delivered to a
central file area by the person who wants to see a file. The
form is used by full-time records employees to locate the
desired file. An example of a requisition form is shown in
Figure 7.1.

Requisitions can also be prepared and delivered by computer. In some organizations, employees gain access
to records using mechanical equipment that delivers records
to them.

Electronic access to records has become the norm in most
large organizations and many small ones. Employees requiring
access to records enter identifying data at their desk terminal.

The desk terminal is part of a *network,* or group of computers linked together electronically, that allows communications with the central database. The requested record appears
on the employee's computer screen. If hard copy is required,
employees print from their screen using their own printer or a
centrally located printer. (In Chapter 11 you will learn about another type of electronic access to records that uses computer
software to track paper, micrographic, and electronic records.)

Documentation is a written account of *who* retrieved a
record and *when* it was retrieved. It is an important part of the
retrieval process. In a small office, it may not be necessary
to document the removal of a file. Other offices may have a

TAB PRODUCTS CO | RECORD RETENTION REQUISITION

DATE / /

| T O | OFFICE SERVICES DEPT. | F R O M | (NAME) |
| | | | (DEPT.) |

☐ TRANSFER RECORDS TO WAREHOUSE FOR STORAGE (FILL OUT COLUMNS 1, 2 & 5 ONLY)

☐ TRANSFER RECORDS FROM WAREHOUSE TO DEPARTMENT (FILL OUT COLUMNS 1, 5 & 6 ONLY)

1	2		3	4	5	6
DESCRIPTION	DATE		CATEGORY NUMBER	DESTRUCTION DATE	BOX NUMBER	STORAGE RACK NC
	FROM	TO				

SEND ALL COPIES OF COMPLETED FORM TO OFFICE SERVICES

WAREHOUSE COPY

FOR OFFICE SERVICES USE ONLY

DELIVERY INSTRUCTIONS: DRIVER PICK-UP _____ BOXES
AMOUNT

FROM: _____
DEPARTMENT / NAME

ON _____
DATE

DELIVER TO: _____
DEPARTMENT / NAME

FORM C-6586

Figure 7-1

Example of a requisition form.

policy to insert an **out guide** in the file in place of a removed record or folder. An out guide, illustrated in **Figure 7.2**, is a heavy paper signpost that documents the location from which the record was removed, the name of the record, the person who borrowed it, and the date it was borrowed. It may also include a column to indicate when the record is due back.

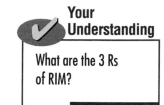

Your **Understanding**

What are the 3 Rs of RIM?

In larger offices, the documentation procedure may be computer-based and produce *by-product information.* By-product information is a group of facts created for a secondary reason. For example, the primary purpose of an access documentation computer program is to ensure the timely return of borrowed records, so the system's primary information will answer the question: Who borrowed what records and when? By-product

OUT			
OUT TO	FILE NUMBER OR NAME OUT	DATE	
ALGO CORP	D JUDD	2/16/--	

Figure 7-2

Example of an Out Guide.

information that can be generated from the same system might answer other questions:

1. Which records are most active?
2. Which records are completely inactive?
3. Who borrows what records?
4. Which records are overdue?
5. Who are the delinquent borrowers?
6. What is the location of all records that have been borrowed?

Delivery is the component of retrieval in which requested records are conveyed to the user. Again, with a small system, the user may perform this job.

With a larger system, a courier service may deliver records. In some businesses, hard copy records that have been requested are copied. The original record is refiled in the records area, and the copy is sent to the user.

In other operations, the requested record is faxed to the user. In neither case does the user necessarily have to return the copy to the records center for destruction.

The copy and fax procedures have two advantages: (1) the original record is always available for others to use, and (2) the next two components of retrieval, follow-up and recovery, can be disregarded.

Electronic delivery is a fast and efficient way to transmit information. In Unit 3, Electronic Information Management, you will learn more about electronic databases and other technology used for electronic delivery.

Follow-up is the component of retrieval in which records employees communicate with users if borrowed records are due. A simple reminder by e-mail, voice mail, or interoffice memo provides two options: return the records or extend the loan period.

Recovery takes place when borrowed records have been returned. Returned records should first be inspected for completeness and possible damage. They should then be refiled, and any manual or computer documentation should note their return.

Five Major Components of Retrieval

- Access
- Documentation
- Delivery
- Follow-up
- Recovery

Retention

Records retention is probably the most complex and difficult issue for the professional records and information manager. Records retention decisions are complicated because the RIM professional is responsible for fashioning reasonable answers to several difficult questions.

Your Understanding

What are the five components of records retrieval?

1. **Use:** How long does the organization require the use of each category of record? It may be difficult for users to agree on the answer. It is the RIM professional's job to negotiate a logical answer and sell it to the users.

2. **Inactivity:** At what point should records be declared inactive? What specific records are considered permanent, never to be destroyed? Should inactive records be transferred to low-cost storage areas, or should they be destroyed and recycled? Only extensive studies and careful cost analyses will reveal answers to these questions.

3. **Laws and regulations:** What federal, state, and local legal requirements for keeping records must be followed? Such requirements are numerous and intricate and can differ from one locality and state to another. For example, a popular book dealing with federal recordkeeping requirements contains more than 1400 laws in a 1300-page, two-volume set (see D.S. Skupsky, *Legal Requirements for Business Records,* Information Requirements Clearinghouse, Englewood, CO., 1992).

4. **Cost:** What is the cost of keeping records versus the cost of not keeping them? As mentioned in Chapter 4, cost figures may be difficult to pinpoint, but it is the RIM professional's job to make informed estimates.

5. **Off-site storage:** Which records, if any, should be transferred to a less expensive or more secure storage location away from the central offices? This question involves, among other things, the issues of access to inactive records, the cost of the off-site storage, and whether or

not inactive records should be filmed or converted to electronic form before they are transferred.

6. **Integrity and security:** Will transferred records maintain their integrity so specific records can be located when needed? Will transferred records be protected properly from destruction and unauthorized use?

Only after the RIM professional has dealt with these and other issues can final decisions related to retention be made.

Not every RIM professional will choose to adopt the following records and information manager's creed, originated by the authors of this textbook. We hope the creed will be helpful for setting the tone for efficient records retention.

The Records and Information Manager's Creed

I believe that . . .

- Most information should not be recorded on paper.
- Most paper records should not be filed.
- Most filed paper records should not be kept for more than one year
- Most paper records kept for more than one year should not be retained in active files.
- Most paper records in inactive files can be destroyed within two to seven years.

Considerations for Retention

- Use
- Inactivity
- Laws and regulations
- Cost
- Off-site storage
- Integrity and security

A precise *retention schedule* might be one result of a well-planned retention policy. Retention schedules are forms that list each type of record and the number of years each is to be retained. The sample retention schedule on page 93 shows how part of an uncomplicated retention schedule might look. These example retention periods may be appropriate only for certain organizations.

RETENTION SCHEDULE

Accounts Payable	Retention Period
Certificates, international import	3 years
Chargebacks	4 years
Check register	4 years
Check requests	4 years
Checks, cancelled	6 years

Accounts Receivable	Retention Period
Accounts charged off	6 years
Aging reports	1 year
Cash receipts journal	2 years
Customer ledger cards or tapes	6 years
Reconciliations	2 years
Statements, monthly	6 years

Advertising	Retention Period
Claims and allowances written off	4 years
Copy (all media)	3 years

Recycling

Records storage is too expensive and cumbersome for organizations to keep all records forever. The vast majority of records must eventually be destroyed and, whenever possible, recycled to protect the environment. Three major considerations in destroying records are cost, security, and environmental protection.

Cost

The least costly way to rid the organization of records is simply to throw them away or deposit them for recycling.

**Recycling
Considerations**

- Cost
- Security
- Environmental
  protection

Records with little or no security requirement may be disposed of in this way.

Security

If security is a factor, the records should be made illegible before they are thrown away. Some companies *incinerate,* or burn, records. This process can be expensive, especially when clean air devices must be installed. Some organizations bury records, but this process is not entirely secure. A *disintegrator* is a machine that chops materials into small pieces. Disintegration provides excellent security but is expensive because of the cost of the equipment. *Pulping* is a process used to destroy records by adding water and creating a slurry mixture. Like disintegration, pulping offers excellent security but the special equipment required is costly. Probably the most popular way to destroy records before they are recycled is shredding. A *shredder,* or shredding machine, like the one shown in **Figure 7.3,** cuts paper into small pieces or strips. The shredded paper

Figure 7-3

Paper shredder. *What issues do you think you should consider when selecting a shredder?*

can be compacted, baled, and recycled. Some powerful shredders can accept file folders, paper clips, staples, credit cards, floppy disks, audio and video CDs, microfilm, ring binders, and telephone books.

Environmental Protection

Recycling and reducing the use of paper saves three of our valuable natural resources: trees, from which paper is made; water, which is required in the manufacture of paper; and landfill space, where used paper is discarded if it is not recycled.

The RIM professional can also help protect the environment by purchasing recycled paper. Improvements in manufacturing recycled paper make it only a little more expensive than virgin paper, and the quality is almost the same. Recycled paper is usually made from about half recycled materials and half new materials. See **Figure 7.4** for an example of a paper recycling system.

Paper is not the only records medium that can be recycled. The RIM professional should also be alert to possibilities for recycling plastic, metal, and glass materials.

Recycling Saves Natural Resources

- Trees
- Water
- Landfill space

Figure 7-4

Recycling system. *What type of recycling system could you set up at home?*

Your Understanding

What are three things to consider when destroying records?

TERMS TO KNOW

▼

1. Review these key terms and important terms.

- **access**
- **by-product information**
- **delivery**
- **disintegrator**
- **documentation**
- **follow-up**
- **incinerate**
- **network**
- **out guide**

- **pulping**
- **recovery**
- **recycle**
- **requisition**
- **retention**
- **retention schedule**
- **retrieval**
- **shredder**

2. Use each key term in a sentence. Underline or italicize each term.

DISCUSSION QUESTIONS

▼

Answer each question as a written assignment or for class discussion. Be concise in your responses.

1. What type of access to records has become the norm in large organizations?

2. What information should be recorded on an out guide?

3. What is the primary purpose of an access documentation computer program?

4. What are two advantages of sending to a requester a photocopy or fax of a record instead of the original?

5. What takes place in the follow-up component of records retrieval?

6. What should be done before returned records are refiled?

7. What is probably the most complex and difficult issue for the RIM professional?

8. Why are records retention laws and regulations difficult to follow?

9. What are three major considerations in destroying records?

10. What are the disadvantages of simply throwing away records?

11. What advantage do incineration, disintegration, pulping, and shredding have in common?

12. What resources are saved by recycling paper?

CRITICAL THINKING

1. **Gather Facts**   Visit a local business, organization, or government agency to find out:

   - How paper records are retrieved.

   - What policies govern retention.

   - Whether or not paper records are recycled when they are no longer needed.

   Write a statement about your findings.

2. **Generalize from Facts**   Develop a written critique of how the office you visited handles the three Rs of records and information management. Using the information in Chapter 7 as a guideline, write a statement about what improvements might be made as well as what practices appear to be exemplary.

3. **Create New Ideas**   Create a policy statement for the office you visited that addresses specific practices related to retrieval, retention, and recycling.

NETWORKING WITH THE REAL WORLD

Access *College.Grad.Job.Hunter: Your Link to Life After College.* The address is http://www.collegegrad.com/book/contents/. Using the guidelines in this resource, come to class on a date agreed to by your instructor dressed for a successful job interview.

IMPLEMENTING UNIT 2 CONCEPTS

▼

GROUP ACTIVITY

Each member is responsible for providing ten items of paperwork. Do the following at one or more group meetings:

1. Decide which items are records requiring management and which are simply paperwork that may be discarded immediately or after temporary use.

2. For each record kept, make a statement about the consequences if it were discarded.

3. Make a group decision about how each item is to be filed: alphabetically, by subject, numerically, chronologically, or geographically.

4. Index and alphabetize all records that are to be filed alphabetically by the name of a person or organization.

5. Make a group decision about how long each record is to be retained. Suggest how records are to be discarded at the end of the retention period.

6. Write a brief summary report that draws conclusions about the project. Include problems, recommendations, and illuminating factors, such as whether or not the project helped group members analyze some of the challenges of managing paper records.

INDIVIDUAL INQUIRY

Save all of your incoming paper mail and copies of your outgoing paper mail for a week. At the end of the week, count the pieces of paper, not including any incoming mailing envelopes.

- Calculate the percentage of records that you will keep compared to total pages.

- Report the results to your class or to your instructor in the form of a report.

SYNTHESIZING UNIT 2 CONCEPTS

GROUP ACTIVITY

An Associated Press newspaper release reported:

> Every time a patient visits a doctor, it generates seven to ten pieces of paper—even in this age of computer enlightenment.

As a group, you are to 1) investigate the extent to which the problem of paperwork overload in the medical field exists in your locality and 2) make a series of recommendations as to how to solve the problem. You should first identify the problem, then describe possible reasons why the problem exists, and finally identify possible solutions.

Note: Issues you might consider a problem include, but are not limited to, the following:

1. Receipt of hard copy records

2. Creation of hard copy records

3. Indexing and alphabetizing procedures

4. Equipment and supplies for paper records

After you have completed your investigation and analyzed the results, make a series of recommendations as to how to solve the problem. Address the following question in a written or oral report:

What can be done to streamline the administration of health services and medical insurance benefits?

INDIVIDUAL INQUIRY

Address one of these topics in a three- to five-page paper:

1. My theory about the relationship between one's personality type and how that person organizes his or her records.

2. The recycling program in my community.

3. A visit to the landfill.

4. My analysis of the paperwork problems and solutions at [name of business or organization].

ELECTRONIC INFORMATION MANAGEMENT

Three

In Unit 3 you will discover the new world of electronic information management. This unit deals with electronic computer filing systems, database systems, image technology, and automated systems used to manage paper records. Without modern electronic information systems, it would be impossible to manage the millions of records that exist in business, industry, and government today.

PROFESSIONAL PROFILE

LARRY HAYES
Blacksburg, Virginia

Meet **Larry Hayes.** Larry is Vice President and Manager of Information Systems at the National Bank of Blacksburg. Larry manages all areas of electronic technology—the in-house mainframe, local area networks, wide area networks, personal computers, hardware, software, ATMs, and Internet banking—and is responsible for selecting, installing, and supporting all information system projects. He supervises a staff of six individuals who run a 24-hour data processing shop, maintain the computer room, and provide network and personal computer support.

Larry's Career Path. Larry has been in his current position for three years. He began his career with the bank 20 years ago as a computer operator, then worked his way up to Computer Room Supervisor, Data Processing Manager, and Assistant Vice President of Data Processing. Larry has a two-year Programming Certificate from Atlanta Area Technical School. With his past and ongoing experiences, Larry will be prepared to advance to the next level of Senior Vice President.

Managing Electronic Files

The purpose of Chapter 8 is to enable you to:

- Identify the major components of a computer system.
- Differentiate between an operating system and a software application.
- Identify what is needed to create electronic filing systems.
- Name electronic folders and files appropriately using the principles of identification, brevity, and documentation.
- Describe the benefits of entering descriptive information into electronic records using proper records maagement techniques.
- Cite procedures for creating, labeling, and storing backups of electronic records.

KEY TERMS

- application
- backup
- browser
- byte
- CPU
- e-mail
- file
- folder
- hard drive
- hardware
- input device
- operating system
- output device
- program
- root folder

Management of paper records has always been important. In today's workplace, however, many documents are stored in computers. More often than not these documents move from computer to computer and are never printed to paper. Records management professionals must therefore name, file, distribute, and otherwise manage electronic records as well. This chapter provides a basic introduction to computers, in general, and to the creation and management of electronic records, also known as files.

Computer Systems

The vast majority of electronic records are stored on a computer. A *computer* is an electronic device used to create, store, manipulate, and perform calculations on data using a set of instructions. The set of instructions is called a **program.** The power of a computer comes from its ability to execute many different programs. A computer with the correct program can be used to create a report, store it in electronic form, send it to all the members of a department, and secure it so unauthorized people cannot view it.

Computers require three major components: hardware, an operating system, and programs or **applications.**

Information is stored in computers in units called bytes. A **byte** is one character or space. That means the sentence you are now reading contains 62 bytes. The 62 bytes include everything from the T to the ., including the spaces.

Letters, reports, spreadsheets, and other documents contain a large number of bytes. When discussing larger sizes, we use terms such as *kilobyte,* which is equivalent to 1024 bytes. A *megabyte* is equivalent to 1024 kilobytes, or 1,048,576 bytes. A *gigabyte* is 1024 megabytes.

Computer Hardware

Computer **hardware** includes all of the physical parts of the computer, the most important of which are the **central processing unit (CPU),** keyboard, monitor, disk drives, mouse, and printer (see **Figure 8.1**). The brain of the computer is the central processing unit, or CPU. It is responsible for making decisions, performing mathematical calculations, and manipulating electronic data. The rest of the hardware is used to save information or move it into and out of the CPU.

Input devices allow computer operators to enter data into the computer. Examples of input devices are the keyboard, mouse, microphone for dictation, video camera, touch screen, and document scanner. **Output devices** give information back

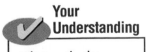

Your Understanding

What are the three major components of a computer?

Figure 8.1

Computer hardware.

to computer operators in a form they can understand. These include the monitor, printer, and speakers.

Storage devices are those parts of the hardware used for holding information in an electronic form until the information is needed by the CPU or by people using the computer. Many varieties of storage devices are used. Each has a different purpose that depends on whether or not it can be removed from the computer and what amount of information it can store. **Table 8.1** is a list of storage devices, their general size, and their uses.

Figure 8.2

3.5″ floppy disks.

Computer Hardware

- Central processing unit (CPU)
- Input devices (keyboard, mouse, microphone)
- Output devices (monitor and printer)
- Storage devices (disks and tapes)

Table 8.1 Storage Devices

Type	Amount of Data It Can Hold	Permanent or Removable	Uses
Floppy disk **(Figure 8.2)**	Very small amount	Removable	Temporary storage of small data files. Used to move information from one computer to another when other means are not available.
Hard drive (or hard disk)	Very large amount	Permanent	Stores the operating system, application programs, documents, and records used by a computer on a regular basis.
CD-ROM (compact disk-read only memory	Large amount	Removable (but not recordable)	Stores applications and databases. Mass distribution of electronic information.
CD-R (compact disk-recordable)	Large amount	Removable (record once)	Stores large documents and databases. Used to create permanent electronic archives.
Tape	Very large amount	Removable	Creates copies of hard drive information to protect from loss due to theft or damage.

- Microsoft Windows 98
- Apple OS9
- Linux
- Solaris
- OS/2
- VMS

Programs or applications that can run with one operating system usually cannot run with others.

Operating Systems

Because the hardware consists of many different pieces of physical equipment connected together, the computer requires a special program that allows each of those pieces to communicate and work together. This special program is called an **operating system.**

An operating system provides a consistent way for an application program to talk to each piece of hardware that it needs. By managing the applications and the hardware, it enables the person using the computer to do more than one task at a time. You can edit a document while you print out a spreadsheet.

An operating system also provides one more vital function: it creates an electronic filing system so many different applications and documents can be stored on the computer's storage devices in a logical way.

Software Applications

An **application** is a program or group of programs for doing a specific task or set of tasks. Some are used for creating written documents such as this textbook. Others are used to perform financial calculations, manipulate pictures, calculate the thrust required for a rocket to reach orbit, manage property, or run a manufacturing operation.

Electronic Filing Systems

**Your
Understanding**

What is the difference between an operating system and an application?

An *electronic filing system* is the combination of the computer hardware, operating system, and software that allows information to be stored and organized in a logical and usable way. Each of the computer's storage devices is organized using the operating system's filing system. The electronic filing system maintains a list of all files and their location. By understanding how these filing systems work, you can manage all of the computer's information logically and consistently.

Files and Folders

All computers store applications, documents, and other information as files. A **file** is an electronic record that has a name and is treated as a single item, like a book, that has certain capabilities and is stored in a single place. A file is located in a **folder** (also called a *directory*), which is the computer's equivalent of a file drawer. Folders also have names and locations like files. A folder can contain files and other folders. There is no limit to the number of folders you can open before reaching a certain file. This means that folder **A** can contain folder **B,** which contains folder **C,** which contains folder **D** (see Figure 8.3).

Root Folder

All files are contained within a folder. Most folders are also contained within another folder. However, some folders stand on their own. These are called root folders or root directories.

A **root folder** is accessed directly without the need to access any other folders. In the Microsoft Windows operating system, the disks themselves act as root folders; these disks are usually named with letters of the alphabet. The A: root

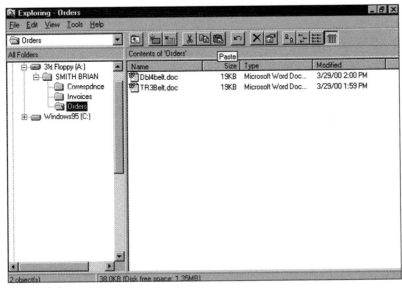

Figure 8.3

Folders, subfolders, and files in drive A.

folder (also called the A: drive) is always a floppy disk. The C: root folder is on a hard drive. Drive letters on Windows systems can be labeled through the alphabet.

Organizing Electronic Files

Because computers today can store millions of different files, logical organization is essential. Once a logical structure for storing files has been established, all members of an organization will be able to save or retrieve documents efficiently.

Logical Organization of Folders

The most important rule to remember in organizing electronic files is that the same methods that work with paper also apply to computers. In other words, create folders (directories) that make sense from a logical or organizational perspective. For example, if your business or organization is a global enterprise and files paper records using a geographic filing system, then the computer's folders should be set up using a geographic system.

Folders created from the root should be the most general. In the example in **Figure 8.4** the top-level folders are sales regions. Within each of the general folders, folders containing more specific geographic references are created. Figure 8.4 shows states within each sales region. Within each state folder, a set of city or district folders is created. Within those we could have folders for each quadrant of the city, or for each salesperson, or for individual clients.

One of the advantages of an electronic system is that the number of subdivisions of documentation is almost endless. In the above example, we could instead have a folder for each client, then each product category for the client, then each product line, then each sale, then break that into administrative areas such as "Bids," "Proposals," "Letters," "Contracts," and "E-mail."

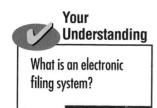

Your Understanding

What is an electronic filing system?

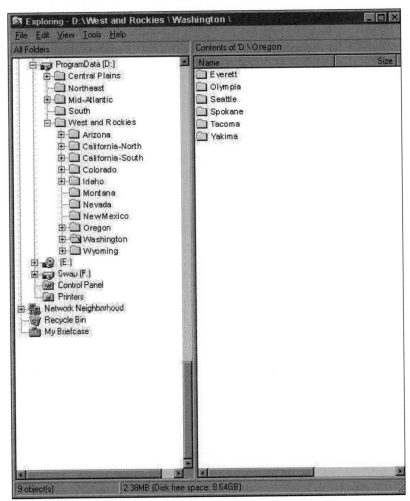

Figure 8.4

Logical folder structure.

Shortcuts

One interesting electronic filing device is a special file whose only purpose is to point to another file. This special file is called a *shortcut* (or *alias* or *link*). A shortcut allows you to develop multiple filing systems for the same files. For instance, for the example in Figure 8.4, we could develop a completely separate structure of folders based on a subject-based filing system. Each of the folders in the subject-based system would have shortcuts pointing to the records that are stored in the geographic-based folders. Shortcuts are used so there is only one copy of each electronic record in the system. Shortcuts should remind you of cross-referencing, which was discussed in Chapters 5 and 6. In this case, the shortcut is an electronic cross-reference between the subject-based and the geographic-based information.

PROBLEM Michael Rabinowitz was put in charge of the computer-based files in the sales department of Acme Machine Company. His boss told him that his first job was to create a new filing system. The current system is based on the geographic arrangement of the sales force. Now, a customer-based system is desired. Michael must create a folder structure that uses major customer categories, customer names, and sales contacts. However, it was decided that the old system should also be left in place so other office staff could change to the new system over time.

Michael spent several days planning a completely new set of folders using file naming principles discussed on pages 112–115. He carefully documented the structure to inform the staff. Once finished, Michael placed in the new filing system a copy of each of the files in the old system, giving them the same names.

Several weeks later, Michael's boss called him into the office. Apparently, several salespeople had been using files with old prices and had not been able to find the up-to-date proposals that their partners had been working on. Why?

Some of the staff was using the old system, while others were using the new system. Michael did almost everything right. The problem is that when he made the new folders, he placed duplicate copies of the old files in them instead of creating shortcuts to the old files. To the computer, a copy is a completely different file, whether it has the same name or not. Some of the staff was using the new folder layout to make changes to proposals and price sheets. Others were using the old layout and getting price lists that had not been changed.

With shortcuts, the problem of outdated price lists and proposals would be eliminated because there is only one file. When a person uses the new system, he or she is opening the file stored in the old system. When changes to prices and proposals are made and saved, they are visible to everyone, no matter whether they are using the old folder system or the new.

File Names and File Types

It is easy to get confused about naming files because each operating system has different rules. Older systems require that the file name be only a few characters and that all of the characters be alphanumeric (A–Z or 0–9). Other systems allow longer names and more characters (such as #, _ , - , and @) but do not allow spaces in the file names. Windows 95 improved the situation by allowing long file names that can contain almost any character you can type on your keyboard.

You should consult your computer's manual before assigning a name to your files. Because there are so many different rules, this book will concentrate on the naming rules and conventions of the Microsoft family of operating systems (Windows 95, Windows 98, Windows NT, and Windows 2000).

File Name Requirements

A *file name* is the caption you assign to an electronic record or document. It identifies the computer record like a caption in a paper file identifies the paper record. No two file names in the same electronic file folder may be exactly the same. Without a unique file name, it would be impossible to locate and retrieve an electronic file.

Beginning with Windows 95 and the introduction of long file names, the ability to give files descriptive names became much easier. But, this freedom can lead to another problem—file names that are too long. The ability to have long file names does not make the naming of files a trivial task. It does, however, give the flexibility to add identifying information such as version numbers and the creation date to a file name.

For computers using Microsoft Windows, file names:

- May have up to 255 characters total (file name plus file type).
- May consist of any characters except the following:

      >   <   \   /   "   *   ? | :

- May use spaces; however, some applications may not be able to use files that have spaces in the name.

Folder names and file names follow the same rules except that folder names do not have a file type.

In Microsoft Windows, there are two parts to the file name. The first part is the name that you give the file. The second part, called the *file type*, is also called the file extension. The file type helps the computer to understand what program or programs will be able to read the file. A file type is usually assigned by the software application that was used to create it. The operating system uses the file type to *associate* this application with the file. For example, Microsoft Word appends *.doc* to documents created using it. The *.doc* is a period (called a "dot") followed by a two to four-character extension showing that this file is a Microsoft Word document. A *.xls* indicates the document is a spreadsheet created by Microsoft Excel.

EXAMPLE Judith Bancroft has used Microsoft Word to create a letter to send to a client. She has named the file based on the date and the subject of the letter and put it into a folder for the client. The file name she chose is *Recommendation for Purchase - 12Nov2001*. Now that she has completed her work and saved it, the file exists in the computer and is called *Recommendation for Purchase - 12Nov2001.doc*. In a few days Judith can open her file browser (Windows Explorer or My Computer) and double click on *Recommendation for Purchase - 12Nov2001*. Her actions will start Microsoft Word and present this file for editing. Windows looks up the file type in a table to see if a program creates files of this type. Because it does, Windows will run the associated program, Microsoft Word, with the chosen file.

Principles of File Naming

As we have already learned, it is possible to create long file names. However, because it is possible to have a 255-character file name does not mean you should attempt to reach that limit. You should follow three basic principles in naming files: identification, brevity, and documentation.

PRINCIPLE OF IDENTIFICATION If the file name describes the contents of the file briefly, it will be easier to find than if the file name is an abstract code or if it is lengthy. For example, a word processing file might be a bid for construction of the new Stoneville library. A file name such as *Stoneville Lib Bid.doc* would be easier to find than *Stoneville Library Construction Bid.doc* or *SLC Bid.doc.* When using names or places in the file name, you should follow the same rules you use with paper files. If you transpose names of individuals to label paper records, then the file name you would assign to a letter to John E. Smith would be *Smith John E.letter.doc*

Sometimes it is convenient to include the date as part of the file name. A file **browser** application like Windows Explorer or My Computer, which allows you to see all of the root folders and their folders and files, will show the date that the file was last modified. This date does not necessarily have anything to do with the document date. For instance, you might begin writing a proposal on July 3 and complete it on August 14. If the proposal's effective date is September 1, then the date you should include in the file name is Sept. 1. An addendum may be made to the proposal on October 5. Windows Explorer would now show the date modified as October 5, but you would still want the Sept. 1 notation as part of the file name.

PRINCIPLE OF BREVITY Even though we want the file name to carry enough information for anyone in the office to identify it easily, it should also be kept short enough to fit in a typical file browser window. Twenty characters (before the file type) is a reasonable maximum but not necessarily an absolute maximum. Keeping the file name brief but complete requires that you choose key words or obvious abbreviations from a basic description of the document.

For example, a database containing the inventory of the Westside Warehouse might have the name *Westside inv.mdb* (where .mdb is the file type associated with Microsoft Access). In this example, *Warehouse* is left out and is assumed. Only the location is listed. *Inv* is a reasonable abbreviation for inventory. There is also no need to explain that it is a database.

Assigning File Names

- Principle of identification
- Principle of brevity
- Principle of documentation

You can abbreviate the contents of a file name and still make it descriptive by omitting vowels and unnecessary words and repeating consonants. A few examples follow:

Contents	Principle of Brevity
Customer survey proposal	Cust survey
Architectural specifications for Highwoods Complex	Highwoods spec
Letter to Charles Renault	Renault
This year's budget presentation	Budget pres 2001

File Identifiers

By:
- Name
- Date
- Author
- Chronological sequence
- Type
- Importance
- Retention period
- Destruction date
- Version
- Security level
- By subject

PRINCIPLE OF DOCUMENTATION When choosing a file name for correspondence or other documents that occur many times, such as letters to one client or quarterly budgets, you should include items in the file name that document it completely. The most common way to identify a file is by its name, but other means include the date, author, chronological sequence, type, importance, retention period, destruction date, version, security level, and subject. Because you want to limit the length of file names, only one or two of the documentation factors should be used for one file name. Some examples of documenting the contents of a file in its file name follow:

- Distinguish letters to John E. Smith by including the date and the author. *SMITH JOHN E LTR SMW 011130.doc* identifies this letter as the one written on Nov. 30, 2001, by Stephen M. Williams.

- The quarterly budget for the second quarter of 2001 could be named *Q2 2001 Budget.xls.*

- Document the number of an item of correspondence in chronological order. *Calvert 028* represents the twenty-eighth item of correspondence to Calvert Company.

- Document the classification of a file. A memorandum file name might end with *MEM;* a report, *RPT;* a letter, *LTR;* and a manuscript, *MAN.*

- Document the importance of the file, the period of retention, or the date of destruction. A file that is considered permanent might end with *PRM*. A file to be kept for six months might end with *6MO*. A file to be destroyed at the end of a specific year might end with *D98* or *X98*.

- Document the file version: *D1* for the first draft, *D2* for the second draft, *DF* for the final draft.

- Document the security level of the file. Security levels often indicate which employees are permitted access. A security level of 1 might mean only top management has access to that file; 2, top and middle management; and 3, all administrative staff. Therefore, the file names for the three security levels might end with *S1*, *S2*, and *S3*.

- Document the subject of a file. For example, a sales report may have *SLS*; a manufacturing report, *MAN*; a financial report, *FIN*; and a training report, *TRNC*.

Your Understanding

What are the three basic principles of assigning file names?

Metadata

Metadata is a scientific term for the description of a document. This descriptive information is typically added to the document through the application used to create it rather than as part of the file name or part of the actual document. It is like having a page in a file folder that describes its creator, purpose, and contents. For example, in Microsoft Word there is an item under the File menu called Properties. When you open the Properties box, you will see several items that help identify the document and how it has been used recently. Some of these items are generated automatically when the document is created, such as:

- *Author:* the log-in name of the person who created the document. Your log-in name is your user name associated with your computer. If you work for a company, you must log in when you start work and turn on your computer by entering your user name and password. On your home computer, your user name was set up when you first registered your computer.

- *Last access date:* the last time the file was opened, whether the file was changed or not.
- *Last modify date:* the last time the file was changed.
- *Creation date:* the date the file was originally created.
- *Revision number:* the number of times the document has been changed since it was created.

Other metadata can be added by the author of the document:

- *Title:* a more descriptive title than that used in the file name.
- *Subject and Category:* these descriptive items might be defined by your organization.
- *Manager:* the management person responsible for the document.
- *Keywords:* words that associate the document with related information such as projects, customers, and vendors.

Although the metadata associated with a document is not part of the document itself, it can be a powerful tool when searching for electronic material.

Microsoft Office Metadata

General
- File name
- File type
- Creation date
- Last modification date
- Last print date
- Size

Summary
- Title
- Subject
- Author
- Manager

- Company
- Category
- Keywords
- Comment
- Hyperlink base

Statistics
- Last author
- Number of changes
- Number of pages, words paragraphs, etc.

Custom
- User set metadata

Retrieving Electronic Files

There are two methods of retrieving documents on your desktop computer for viewing and modifying.

1. *You can start the application you will use to view or modify the document.* Then you can "open" the document by selecting the correct folder and file. Microsoft Office products provide features that help in locating documents. Because all Office applications include a "Properties" section containing metadata, you can use the "show properties" option, shown in **Figure 8.5,** to see information about the documents. There are advantages in being diligent about including metadata such as the subject of a document and keywords.

   Also, at the bottom of Figure 8.5 you will see that there is a section that allows you to find files by specifying file names, text, dates, or types of files.

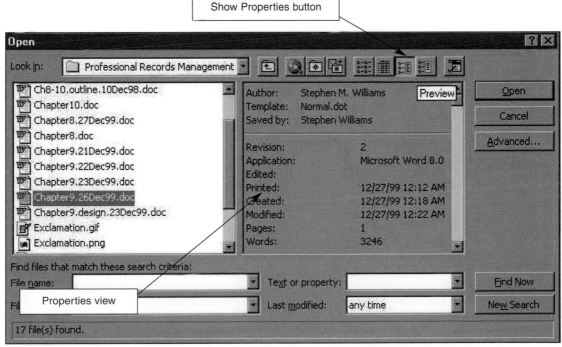

Figure 8.5

Microsoft Word file browser with properties.

Figure 8.6 shows an example of using the Advanced Search feature to look for any Microsoft Word file in the D: drive that has the following *criteria,* or requirements:

- File name includes *quote*
- Can be any file (not just Microsoft Word files)
- Uses the keywords *west, coast,* and *appliance*
- File modified within the last month
- Has the word *report* as part of the subject

In this example, these requirements were *AND*ed together, which means that all the criteria must be met to retrieve the file. You can also use an *OR* for the criteria, which will show documents if any one of the criteria are met.

2. *You can use the operating system tools, such as your file browser, to locate the document and open it using its associated application.* One of the basic tools in the

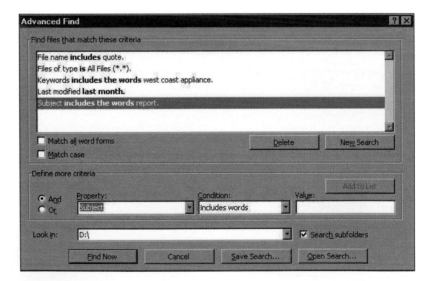

Figure 8.6

Microsoft Word Advanced Search

Microsoft Windows operating systems for locating a document is Windows Explorer. This application provides a view of the electronic file system showing the root file at the top and its folders beneath it. Windows Explorer lets you use folder names, folder levels, and file names to locate the proper document. It also has a Find tool, which is similar to the Microsoft Office Advanced Search window except that you can search all files in the file system. With the Find tool, you can look for files with a particular name (or part of a name), you can specify the date of the last modification, and you can specify text contained anywhere in the document.

Figure 8.7 shows a Find search in which the user wishes to locate any document on the D: drive containing the word *electronic*. (Performing this operation on a full hard drive may take a long time because the operating system must open and examine the contents of every file.)

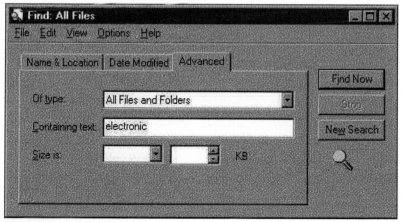

Figure 8.7

Conducting a Find Search.

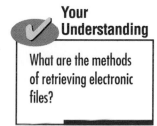

Your Understanding

What are the methods of retrieving electronic files?

Presenting Electronic Information

Electronic records are usually presented to people other than their creators. Sometimes a document is presented to a customer, vendor, or other group outside your organization or company. Sometimes it is presented to people within the company.

Recipients Outside Your Organization

A common way to send documents to people outside your organization is to send them an electronic mail, or **e-mail,** message. E-mail applications allow you to include electronic documents as attachments to an e-mail message. When you use the attachment capability, you will be presented with a browser from which to select the folder and document you wish to send. The attached document will be a copy of your document. The attachment will not be part of your e-mail message; it must be opened separately by the recipient.

When letters, contracts, and other records are sent to customers or vendors, they are often given a unique document number for tracking purposes. A *tracking number* is a unique identifier assigned so that both the sender and the recipient can be sure they are referring to the same document. When a tracking number is used, it should appear in the electronic record either as part of the file name or in the metadata. Examples of document tracking numbers appear in the chart on page 121 **(Figure 8.8).**

When sending records to customers or vendors electronically, certain precautions should be taken:

- Make a copy of the file in a temporary location and change the name of the copy to the document tracking number. You can delete this copy after you send it because it is a *copy*—the original file will still exist with its internal file name.
- Do not send "marked-up" files. With Microsoft Office products, you can set a feature called "Track Changes" to keep track of changes made to the document. This feature

Tracking Number	Description
VT01110322	Company abbreviation followed by the date as YYMMDD and a document number (the twenty-second document of the day)
34599923 SW	Sequential document number followed by the author's initials
2001-2345-VT-5-SW	Year; document number 2345 for the year; customer abbreviation; revision number; author initials

Figure 8.8

Examples of document tracking numbers.

is useful to you, but it should not be seen by your customer or vendor.

- If the document is a legal document (such as a contract or price quote), it should be sent in a format that cannot be edited. You should also include a *digital signature* if possible. A digital signature is the digital equivalent of a signature. It can be placed on a document by a special application program that creates a unique string of digits that can be identified by the recipient if he or she has a program to interpret it. This feature allows the recipient to verify the source of the document. The digital signature can also be used to give you control over how the document is used. For example, you can allow it to be viewed but not printed.

Recipients Within Your Company or Organization

There are three possible ways to send a document to someone within your organization. Each of these methods has certain advantages; each also has certain rules that should be followed to allow the recipient to handle the document properly.

**To Send a
Document
Within an
Organization**

- E-mail attachment
- Pointer or hyperlink
- Hard copy

1. Send it as an *attachment* to an e-mail message. This option gives the recipient a copy of the document that can be viewed, printed, or changed. It is useful when the recipient does not have access to your original document on your computer system.

   - Recipients can store the document on their computer in an appropriate folder, make changes, and send it back if necessary. If both you and the recipient use the same file name, then you will know where to put it when it is sent back.

   - Include explanatory information about the document in the e-mail message. For example, you might include in the e-mail message the name of the folder that holds the document.

   - If the application used to create the document allows you to track changes, turn this feature on. You and the recipient can thus see any changes that were made to the original document.

2. Send a pointer to the document. A *pointer* or *hyperlink* acts like the shortcut discussed earlier in this chapter. It allows you to jump to another location, such as another file on your hard disk, your company's network, or an Internet address. Instead of sending a copy of the file, you send a pointer that allows the recipient to make changes to the actual document. The recipient must have access to the document in its current location in the computer system.

   - If the application allows you to track changes, turn that feature on so the changes are visible to both you and the recipient.

   - If the application allows more than one person to edit the document at once, turn on this feature. You and your coworker can thus make changes to the same document simultaneously without causing the file to be corrupted, or made illegible. (If you use this feature, you should coordinate who will work on each section of the document, and you should save your work often. If two or more people change the same part of the document between saves, it will be necessary to decide which change to accept when saving the document.)

3. Print a hard copy of the document and send or give it to your coworker. This method is convenient if the recipient does not plan to change the document or does not have access to an electronic version. A paper copy is also desirable when you intend to present information from the document at a meeting.

Long-term storage requirements for certain documents may require that you print a paper copy for archival purposes. When you print paper copies, you should:

- Include the full file name in the page header or footer. This feature provides a way to access the electronic version of the document.

- Print the date and time in the header or footer of the document. This information gives recipients the ability to determine the age of the printed copy.

- Print the page number on each page. An electronic document always remains as one unit. The same cannot be said of multipage paper versions.

Whenever you present a copy of any electronic record to another party, you should keep track of who has received it so you know who should receive updated versions. This information gives you an audit trail, which is a way of tracking what has happened to the record.

Principles for Backups of Electronic Records

As with important paper documents, storage and protection of electronic records is of paramount importance in any organization. Because electronic storage devices can be corrupted or damaged and because it is easy to destroy documents accidentally, computers should have their contents copied regularly onto a more permanent medium. This procedure is called a **backup.** All documents on a computer should be backed up at least once a month if records do not change often, or once a week or even once a day if the computer is used regularly. Several types of storage media are available for keeping backups of important files:

- **Tapes:** A tape is the most common storage medium. It can hold an enormous amount of information and is inexpensive.
- **CD-R disks:** A recordable CD can hold up to 650 MB, and its contents can be loaded easily onto nearly any computer.
- **Another computer:** Another computer is a typical means of holding information that must be easily accessible but is also too valuable to entrust to a single computer.

Labeling Backups

When backups are made, each tape or disk should be labeled appropriately. The label should clearly state the following information:

- Date
- Total number of tapes or disks in the collection
- Number of each tape or disk in the sequence
- Computer being backed up
- Contents of the backup (one file, a group of folders, the entire hard drive)

- Type of backup

  A backup can be one of two types:

  1. A *full backup* contains complete copies of every file. If a file is lost or if the computer's disk becomes corrupted or illegible, the data can be retrieved from this backup.

  2. An *incremental backup* contains only the changes since the last incremental or full backup **(Figure 8.9)**. For large computer systems, this method provides a way to avoid using dozens of tapes or disks every time a backup is done. However, it also means that in the event of a computer failure, the last full backup and each incremental backup recorded after it must be used to restore an electronic file. Incremental backups usually follow a procedure like:

     - Full backup on Mondays
     - Incremental backup on Tuesday through Friday

The following chart gives two examples of backup media labels:

Code	Description
Server: Full Backup Nov 12, 2001 Drives C/D/F Tape 4 of 6	A computer called Server was backed up on November 12, 2001. The backup set contains the complete contents of the C, D, and F drives on the Server computer. The backup set contains six tapes. This is the fourth tape.
2000-04-11-1/2 I Buffy1 D:\user*	The backup was made on April 11, 2000. This is tape one of two in an incremental backup of the D:\user folder and all its contents on the computer named Buffy1.

Types of Backup

- Full backup
- Incremental

Figure 8.9

Examples of backup media labels.

TERMS TO KNOW

▼

1. Review these key terms and important terms.

alias	e-mail	link
AND	file	megabyte
application	file name	metadata
associate	file type	operating system
attachment	folder	OR
backup	full backup	output device
browser	gigabyte	pointer
byte	hard drive	program
computer	hardware	root folder
CPU	hyperlink	shortcut
criteria	incremental backup	software
digital signature	input device	storage device
directory	kilobyte	tracking number
electronic file system		

2. Assume that each key term is the answer to a question. Write a question for each answer.

DISCUSSION QUESTIONS

▼

Answer each question as a written assignment or for class discussion. Be concise in your responses.

1. Explain what computer hardware is and give some examples of computer hardware.

2. Explain what folders or directories are.

3. Your company sells insurance. Company documents are organized by insurance types—whole life, term life, automobile, and homeowners. Give an example of a logical structure of the folders as they would be set up on your computer's network (h:\) drive and how you would file a police report on a traffic accident that involved your policyholder, Sid Kopecky. *Note:* Set up any necessary folders, beginning with the root folder, h:\. Review Logical Organization of Folders on page 108.)

4. Explain what metadata is and why it is useful in finding files.

5. Explain each of the three principles of file naming. Give examples to support the explanation of each principle.

6. Using the three principles of file naming, determine proper file names for the following files:
   a. A letter recommending Anthony Spears for a records management position.
   b. A letter to a vendor, Comstock Electronic Systems, asking for a quote on a new phone system.
   c. The preliminary analysis for charging late fees to customers whose payments are received late.
   d. Your presentation to the director of marketing on your proposed new line of electronic toys for the fall.

7. Name two methods of retrieving electronic files for viewing and modification.

8. What are three ways to send a document to a coworker within your company or organization?

9. Explain why it is important to back up electronic records. How often should backups be done?

CRITICAL THINKING

1. **Gather Facts**   From an office that uses computers at your school or college, determine what rules or protocols are followed in creating file names. Determine if any problems exist regarding the creation and use of file names.

2. **Generalize from Facts**   Write a statement that compares your findings with the principles of file naming presented on pages 112–115.

3. **Create New Ideas**   Write a statement that might be used in your school or college as a guideline for naming files and folders.

NETWORKING WITH THE REAL WORLD

Access http://webopedia.internet.com/TERM/e/ electronic_commerce.html to find and report a definition of e-commerce (electronic commerce).

CHAPTER 9

Using Electronic Databases

The purpose of Chapter 9 is to enable you to:

- Define computer terminology related to electronic database systems.
- Identify the types of hardware and software required to create a database.
- Identify the components of a database.
- Indicate strategies for planning and developing a database.
- Describe how a relational database works.

KEY TERMS

- database
- database management system (DBMS)
- date
- field
- key
- link
- logical
- memo
- number
- query
- record
- relational database
- report
- string
- table

Although many electronic records are stored as files, much of the information used in business today is stored in an electronic system that allows the information to be retrieved or displayed in a wide variety of ways. This system is called a database. Databases are very different from other types of records (paper or electronic). They are different because they do not use traditional paper or electronic files. This chapter deals exclusively with **database management.** The management of database information involves applying rules for organizing the information and creating questions that list the information wanted. You will find that proper management of a database is both challenging and rewarding.

Database Basics

Companies use massive quantities of raw data to provide information for effective decision making. These data are often put into a database. A **database** is a body of organized data, usually managed in a computer system, that can be modified, reorganized, and accessed in various ways to carry out administrative tasks and to solve business problems. Most organizations use databases to store data about their customers, inventory or products, and employees.

Your Understanding

What is a database?

Hardware

Databases are becoming much more common as computers become more powerful. Nearly any computer can support a good database. Some large databases are stored on mainframe computers and are accessed by many workers through a network. Smaller databases might be stored on a desktop computer and are available only to the computer operator. Regardless of the type of computer, the minimum hardware requirements for a database are a central processing unit (CPU), a disk drive, a monitor, and a keyboard. A printer and a mouse are usually also part of the equipment.

If the database is accessed via a network, the computer holding the database acts as a server. A *server* is a computer that holds a company's data and "serves" all the employees who access that data from their individual desktop computer. A network database also requires network hardware and software, as discussed in Chapter 10.

Database Hardware

- Central processing unit (CPU)
- Disk drive
- Monitor
- Keyboard
- Printer
- Mouse

Software

A **database management system (DBMS)** is required for the creation of a database. A DBMS is a computer application package that allows you to create and use a database. Through a DBMS, data can be added to or deleted from a database, changed, sorted, searched for, retrieved, and printed. Calculations can be done, and graphs and charts can be drawn.

Desktop database systems are intended to be used in smaller office settings, with one to ten people accessing the database at a time. Desktop DBMSs are also relatively easy to use. Some desktop DBMSs are:

- Microsoft Access
- Corel Paradox
- Microsoft FoxPro
- Borland dBase

Large databases are designed to run on large network servers and can handle tens of thousands of accesses at once. Some large DBMSs are:

- Microsoft SQL-Server
- IBM DB/2
- Oracle 8

Planning and Developing Databases

Database design takes careful planning. A designer must consider all the data that will be stored, how it will be accessed, and how each piece of data relates to the others.

Designing the Database

Proper database design is crucial to database development. The important question to ask is, "Who is going to use the database and for what purposes?" Employees of a company have different views of how to use the company's data. For example, a sales manager uses the sales data to determine the numbers and amounts of sales, whereas the chief accountant uses some of the same data to determine the income and expenses of the company. The database should be designed so data needed by all employees are considered. The data must be entered into the database so it can be accessed conveniently and understood easily by all who will use it.

Each user is concerned with how the data relate to his or her own job. Workers in the payroll department will view employee data in terms of the number of hours worked and the rate of pay of each employee. People in human resources are also interested in employee pay but not in details about the number of hours worked. They are more interested in keeping

Your Understanding

What must be considered when designing a database?

track of who does what job in what department, what the basic salaries or wages are for different types of jobs, and what job vacancies exist (see **Figure 9.1**).

Components of a Database

The data in a database are organized in a hierarchy of these components: fields, records, and tables. Several fields make a record, and several records make a table.

FIELDS   A **field** is the most fundamental part of a database. It is one category for information storage that cannot be broken down any further. For example, an employee database usually includes a field for a social security number. Other fields might include phone number, name, and address.

Department Head	Type of Information Needed
Marketing Director, Marion Mogul	Name of customer (business name) Address of customer (mailing address) Name of principal contact within the business Types of forms normally ordered Quantities of forms normally ordered Customer's credit rating
Accounting Director, Shad Berkowitz	Name of customer (business name) Address of customer (mailing address) Quantity of forms ordered (for billing) Prices of forms ordered (for billing) Previous balance due Customer's credit rating Credit terms Amount due
Shipping Director, Leslie Popek	Name of customer Ship-to address Types of forms ordered (for filling the order) Quantity of each form type ordered

Figure 9.1

Type of information required by different departments of Wu Business Forms Company.

Database Components

- Fields
- Records
- Tables

Maintenance files for equipment have fields for serial number, purchase date, and service contract number.

Each field has a name that you assign to it when you develop the database **(Figure 9.2)**. Field names should follow the same rules used for other labeling. They should be descriptive but short. You should keep field names simple and use only alphabetic characters and numbers (do not use other characters or spaces). Often one database will get its information from a different database, or a small database may be incorporated into a large database system. If the field names do not follow the rules of the system to which the data are being sent, the field names may be changed to nonsensical titles. Using a field-naming scheme that reflects the rules of most databases reduces that possibility. See Figure 9.2 for examples.

Not only do fields have names, they also have a *type* that must be specified when the database is created. A field may be one of the types described in the following sections.

NUMBER   Any numeric value that you intend to use in mathematical equations must be declared as a **number** type. A number can contain the digits 0 through 9 or a combination of digits such as 82 or 2750. Numeric fields may also contain a decimal point and/or a minus sign. **Figure 9.3** shows four number examples. With some database software, you may be required to choose a maximum size for your number. If so, you must decide if it will be an *integer,* which is a whole number, or *real,* which indicates that it can have fractions. Number sizes and their ranges are shown in **Figure 9.4.**

LastName	PatientID	HomePhone	VisitDate

Figure 9.2

Sample field names.

QuantityOnHand	AnnualSalary	DiscountAmt	SalesToDate
46152	38950	−45.50	271336.17

Figure 9.3

Sample number fields.

Specifying a field as a number type will allow you to use mathematical equations. For example, you may wish to multiply the price of a product by the number of items to calculate the total cost. **Figure 9.5** displays some sample numbers that can be entered in a field specified as a number type.

STRING OR ALPHANUMERIC   A **string** field type is any collection of *alphanumeric* characters. This means that a string can be a word, a sentence, a phrase with numbers, or a number by itself. Strings can include alphabetic characters, numbers, and other keyboard characters such as #, @, $, %, &, _, -, +, ?, >, and <. Most of the fields you create will be specified as strings. When you store a string in a field, it will always be treated as an indivisible unit. Therefore, if you want to sort addresses by street name, for example, you should store the name and house number in separate fields, *even if they are both stored as strings.* **Figure 9.6** shows examples of string or alphanumeric fields.

Many field entries that you might think of as numbers should be stored in a database as a string. For example, because

Number Size	Integer or Real	Minimum Value*	Maximum Value*
Byte	Integer	0	255
Integer (or short)	Integer	−32,768	32,767
Long integer	Integer	−2,147,483,648	2,147,483,647
Single (or real)	Real	−3.402823 E38	3.402823 E38
Double	Real	−1.79769313486231 E308	1.79769313486231 E308
*E is an exponential number ($2.5E3 = 2.5 \times 10^3 = 2500$).			

Figure 9.4

Number sizes and ranges.

34	23.45	2.34E−4	.0000234

Figure 9.5

Sample numbers.

Field Name	Field Entry
FirstName	Josephine
LastName	Smith
StreetAddress	301 S. Main Street
PhoneNumber	(312)555-6773
PatientNumber	2120067
SpecialNotes	Watch patient's liquid and caloric intake. Has lost several #s this week.

Figure 9.6

Sample string or alphanumeric fields.

zip codes and social security numbers (SSNs) are not used in calculations and are sorted and viewed a particular way, they should be stored as strings. **Figure 9.7** shows zip codes sorted incorrectly in the left column because they were stored as numbers.

In the zip code example of Figure 9.7, codes with the four-digit extension are viewed by the computer as very large numbers if they are stored using the number type. The computer would put them at the end of the list when sorting, as shown in the left column. This placement is not the order in which we would usually want the zip codes to be sorted. Sorting zip codes as strings, however, works well whether or not the four-digit extension is included. This sorting of strings is shown in the right column.

In the case of social security numbers, a leading zero is the culprit. Many social security numbers begin with a zero. Leading zeros in number fields are not displayed and are not considered when sorting. Storing the SSN as a string eliminates this problem, as shown in **Figure 9.8.**

In both cases, with zip codes and social security numbers, we also want the ability to display the numbers with hyphens. This option is not possible if the entry is stored in a number field.

Stored as Number	Stored as String
23402	23402
23403	23402-0000
25340	23402-2345
98345	23403
234020000	25340
234022345	98345

Figure 9.7

Sorting zip codes.

Stored as Number	Stored as String
10334030	010-33-4030

Figure 9.8

Social security number display.

Another consideration in using strings is how to designate the length of a field when designing a database. Some fields, such as the abbreviation for a U.S. state, have a known length of two characters. Others can vary greatly, as shown in **Figure 9.9.** If you had determined that twelve characters would be enough space for 90 percent of all street names in the database, then choosing a length of twelve might be sufficient. If

R O B I N _ R D . _ _ _	Okay, room left over
M O R N I N G S T A R	No room for Rd., Dr., Ave., etc.
B L A C K W E L L T O W	Not enough room for name: "Blackwelltown Rd."

Figure 9.9

Sample strings with a length of twelve characters (Name of field is StreetName).

a large percentage of street names (including Rd,. St., etc.) are found to be fifteen characters or more, however, then the length chosen for the field should be fifteen or more.

LOGICAL Some fields require only a yes or no response. These **logical** fields are often shown as a box that allows only the words "Yes" or "No" to be entered (see **Figure 9.10**).

Field Name	Value	Field Name	Value
USCitizen	Yes	Minor	No
PsngrVehicle	Yes	FormerCustomer	Yes

Figure 9.10

Sample logical field names/field entries.

Field Types

- Number
- String
- Logical (yes/no)
- Date
- Memo
- Link

DATE Any field that will contain a date or time should be specified as a **date** field. Functions built into most database software allow you to sort by date or find items:

- Between two dates
- Before a specified date
- Within a certain number of days of a specified date.

Date and time entries can take several forms, as shown in **Figure 9.11.**

MEMO Although strings can be up to 256 characters long, we sometimes want a field to hold several paragraphs of descriptive text. In that case, it should be specified as a **memo** field. A memo field can have up to 65,536 characters (64 kilobytes). Memo fields cannot be sorted and many of the functions that work with string fields will not work with memo fields in most databases.

LINK Although it is desirable to keep all information in the database, sometimes we want to keep a large file, such as

3/4/03	Monday, July 12, 2004	12:30:23 AM	5/4/2001 12:33:44 PM

Figure 9.11

Sample dates.

a video, separate from the database but have it available in records that are sorted and queried. We can accomplish this setup by leaving the large file separate from the database and creating a **link** to it. If these linked files are large, the database speed is enhanced compared with bringing the files into the database itself. However, linking requires that the file referred to in the link can never be moved. If the file is moved or deleted, the database would have a link that refers to a non-existent file.

RECORDS   A database **record** includes all the fields related to *one* customer, employee, vendor, client, person, company, organization, product, case, item, etc. Several examples of records are shown in Figures 9.12 through 9.14. Can you name the type of each field in the records? The four fields in **Figure 9.12** comprise Max Steinberg's *employee record*. The four fields shown in **Figure 9.13** comprise the *inventory record* for the product *steel bench brace*. An example of a *customer record* is shown in **Figure 9.14.**

SSN	Employee Name	Job Title	Start Date
398-12-0895	Max Steinberg	Production Manager	03/19/94

Figure 9.12

Fields in an employee record.

ProductName	ProductNumber	QtyOnHand	QtyOrdered
Steel bench brace	21-9600	1239	500

Figure 9.13

Fields in an inventory record.

CustomerName	AcctNumber	Charge	BalanceDue
Sartaj Sanjay G.	2004-7	Yes	346.29

Figure 9.14

Fields in a customer record.

TABLES A database **table** is a group of records that are related. Whereas a customer record would have several fields such as CustomerName, AcctNumber, and Address, the Customer table would have a record for every customer. In a table, all records have the same set of field names and types. A small *Employee table* is shown in **Figure 9.15**. A small *Client table* is shown in **Figure 9.16.**

Figure 9.17 shows the relationship among fields, records, and tables. Each field contains one piece of information about a person, item, or topic. Each record contains all the fields from *one* person, or item. A table contains a set of related records such as all customers, all stock items, or all sales tickets.

Putting It All Together

When you go to a doctor for the first time, you are asked to fill out a form. The form will ask for your name (last, first, and middle initial) and some other data. Your name will be entered into a database as a field. On the patient form, you will also fill out your address, phone number, insurance information, and maybe descriptions of your prior surgeries.

SSN	EmployeeName	JobTitle	StartDate
398-13-0896	Max Steinberg	Production Manager	03/19/94
487-47-9812	Kenneth Yulick	Graphic Artist	10/06/91
571-02-8735	Mojgan Mohammed	Press Operator II	05/25/92

Figure 9.15

Database Employee table.

ClientNo	ClientName	ClientAddress	ClientCity	ClientState
2378	International Arts Society	582 N. Main St.	Fairfax	VA
2094	Rachael Skin Care Company	14 Grove Ave.	Hyattsville	MD
1589	Kimbel's Department Stores	3204 New York Ave.	Washington	DC

Figure 9.16

Database Client table.

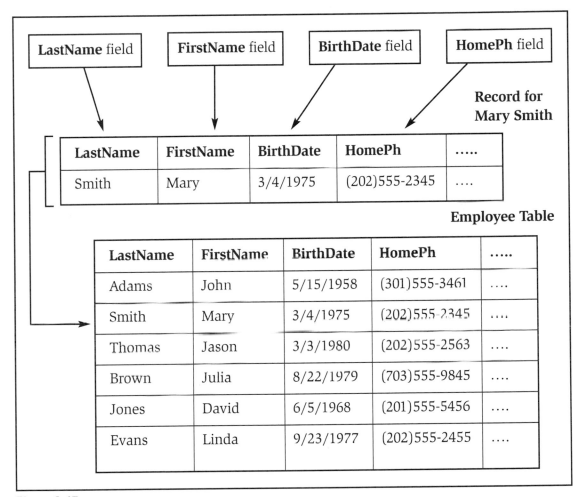

Figure 9.17

Relationship among fields, records, and tables.

When you hand in the form, a technician will enter all that information into a database and thus create your patient record.

Your record is now among all the other patients' records as part of a PatientInformation table. This table will be included in the doctor's database, which may contain other tables such as a patient Visit table and a table containing prescription drugs and their uses.

You may have noticed that nothing was mentioned about how the technician "filed" your patient record. In a database, the records are not stored in any specific order. Your record is simply stored at the end of the table. The next new patient who comes in will be stored after you. This method should make you wonder, "How will they be able to find anything?" This question will be answered later in this chapter when queries are discussed.

Relational Databases

So far, we have seen records built that have one of each type of information: a patient has one last name, one first name, one birthday, etc. You can usually create several tables that work this way. For example, a table that has doctor visit information will have a date, a time of visit, a diagnosis, and a bill amount. When we look at the database, however, we want to be able to see the visits made by a particular patient. How can tables be connected so that we can get only the visits made by Mary Smith?

Most databases today are called **relational databases** because they allow different tables to be related to each other in some way. After you filled out your patient information form, the doctor examined you. The data from this examination was entered into a Visit table. The Visit table is related to the PatientInformation table through a key. A **key** is a unique identifier, such as a patient ID or social security number. Because both the Visit table and the PatientInformation table have a field called PatientID, the DBMS can retrieve information from both tables and show that information at the same time. Each of the records in the Visit table is associated with a corresponding record in the PatientInformation table using the key.

Why don't we put all the information into the same table if it is about the same patient? You have only one identity, but you may visit the doctor many times. One record is created for each office visit. Therefore, if you visit the doctor many times, many "visit" records will be stored. A database saves space by storing only once the data about you that do not change so that by using the key, you can relate that data to the data that *do* change. For example, instead of repeating your name, address, and other data in a new record every time you visit, that information is stored in a separate table. The Visit table will have your patient identification number that relates to the patient

Key field in PatientInformation table

Patient ID	Last Name	FirstName	Street	City
125	Smith	Jane	1 Main St	Leesburg
126	Jones	Davey	12 Elm St	Chester
127	Taylor	Nancy	2023 Duke Dr.	Eastville

Key field in Visit table

VisitID	Patient ID	Date	Symptom	Prescription	Cost
5534	125	2/5/99	Checkup	None	40.00
5535	14	2/5/99	Dizziness	Dramamine	55.00
:	:	:	:	:	:
5834	125	3/15/99	Eye strain	OTC Drops	55.00
:	:	:	:	:	:
6345	125	6/6/99	Back ache	Tylenol 3	55.00
:	:	:	:	:	:
7345	125	2/20/00	Checkup	None	40.00
7346	340	2/20/00	Coughing	OTC syrup	55.00

Figure 9.18

Related tables.

identification number in the PatientInformation table (see **Figure 9.18**). The key in this case is the Patient ID number.

Normalization

To make the database as useful and efficient as possible, a patient's information record, for example, can be split across multiple tables using a process that looks at how each field relates to other fields in terms of the number of possible entries. The goal is to have all fields within a table correspond to the key value of the table on a one-to-one basis. The process of assigning fields to different tables to produce a one-to-one correspondence with each table's key is called *normalization*.

Normalization is best explained through an example. **Figure 9.19** shows some field names in the health care facility's patient information database. By thinking about how each field will be used, we assign patients to one of two tables. One table will have one value per patient, and one will have many values per patient but one for each patient visit (see **Figure 9.20**). Some of the values belong to visits by patients rather than to the patients themselves. The Weight, Height, and BloodPressure of the patients are taken each time they visit and may be different each time. If we had put them in the PatientInformation table, there would be only one per patient and we would not be able to look at a history. The MaritalStatus, on the other hand, may change, but the health care facility probably does not need to know what your marital status was five years ago, so that field can be in the PatientInformation table. By putting these fields into two tables, we have normalized the database.

| LastName | FirstName | Height | Address |
| Weight | BirthDate | BloodPressure | MaritalStatus |

Figure 9.19

Patient database fields

PatientInformation Table (One per Patient)	Visit Table (Many per Patient)
LastName	Weight
FirstName	Height
BirthDate	BloodPressure
Address	
MaritalStatus	

Figure 9.20

Assigning fields to tables.

Relating Tables

Once all our fields and tables have been defined, we need to relate them. In some databases, giving fields in different tables the same name automatically relates them. Usually, however, you must define the relationships for the database. You may also need to tell the computer whether the relationship is one-to-one or one-to-many.

Using the previous example, we can relate the PatientInformation table to the Visit table by the key using a one-to-many relationship—one patient, many visits. In **Figure 9.21,** a relationship window with the three tables is shown. (The ∞ symbol stands for "infinity" or "many" in the database world.) In this example, we have the PatientInformation table whose key is PatientID. Then we have the Visit table that uses the PatientID to relate back to the PatientInformation table. It also has VisitID as its key. Once the doctor has examined you, he or she will prescribe one or more treatments and will record those treatments. Treatment information will be stored in a separate table, the Treatment table. It has a field that relates to the key field in the Visit table. VisitID is used rather than PatientID because each treatment is specific to a particular visit. If PatientID had been used, the the doctor would not be able to tell later when the treatment was prescribed and would lose an important part of your history.

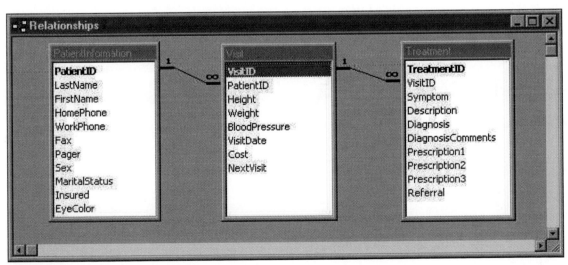

Figure 9.21

Relationships between tables.

Form Design

After the tables have been designed and related to one another, the core of the database is done. Now we must concentrate on entering, changing, and retrieving the data. Although it is possible to enter the information directly into the tables, a table with lots of fields would be extremely difficult to read and use effectively. So we use a window with input fields, check boxes, and drop-down lists to enter and read information. We call this window a *form*. The form can display fields for one record at a time, several records at once, or records from multiple tables.

Figure 9.22 shows a typical form designed using a template and question screens, commonly called a *wizard*. A wizard is a Microsoft Windows feature that allows you to choose the table or tables and lays out each of the fields according to a pattern. In the example of Figure 9.22, the pattern is a columnar view because the data are read from top to bottom. Note that the form allows you to have lists that allow only

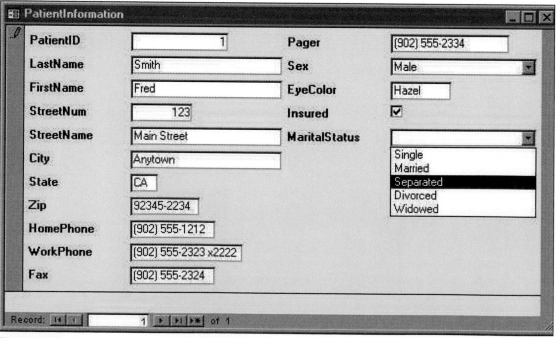

Figure 9.22

Input form in "single record" layout.

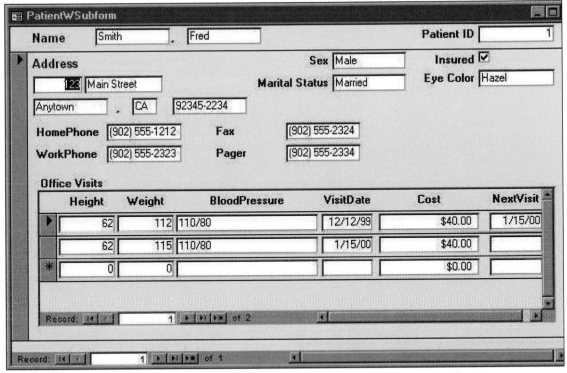

Figure 9.23

Form using information from two tables.

certain choices for items, such as the sex and marital status of the patient.

Figure 9.23 shows a form that contains two tables. The first table is the PatientInformation table and the second is the Visit table. Because there are multiple visits for each patient, it is preferable to display multiple visits on the form. The pattern of this list of visits is called a tabular view because the data are read left to right.

Report Design

Forms are meant mostly for interactive use; in other words, you enter, change, or view the information on a computer screen for one or a small number of records at a time. If you want to view or print information from your database that involves many records, you will want to create a **report**. Creation wizards make it easy to create professional-looking reports from the data in your database.

Queries

Although forms and reports are helpful, the real power of a database comes from its ability to retrieve data that meet your requirements. Using the form in Figure 9.23, you would be able to add new patients or look at each patient one after the other, but you would not be able to find a particular patient with a particular problem.

You can create a set of criteria or rules for finding specific records in your database. These rules force the form or report to show only records that meet those criteria. The selection of records that meet certain criteria is called a **query.** A query is like a mathematical equation; however, this equation can use dates, words, parts of words, or numbers to find records. For example, we can retrieve "all patients with type A blood" or "all customers who live in Santa Fe." The query can give us these records sorted in any number of ways: by zip code, by last name, or by social security number. The management of the information comes through proper entry of information and query construction, rather than through filing and file naming.

For example, a sales representative, Morgan Steinway, receives a phone call from a customer requesting that certain items be shipped as soon as possible. Morgan can immediately search the Customer table for that customer's credit rating to see if shipment can be made prior to payment. Next, the Inventory table can be searched to determine whether all ordered items are in stock. If an item is not in stock, Morgan can tell the customer when to expect shipment. The ability to give the customer information about what will be shipped and when gives the customer confidence in Morgan and the company.

Figure 9.24 shows a query created with the Microsoft Access query wizard for our health care facility example. The query shows that we want to view all visits by people with the last name of Smith that occurred before January 1, 2000.

Figures 9.25 and **9.26** show the results of the query created in Figure 9.24. The Access query first creates temporary records, one for each record in the Visit table. The temporary records use information from the related PatientInformation table in place of PatientID. In this example, there were two visits by Mary Smith, so the patient information about Mary Smith appears in the temporary table twice. After creating the

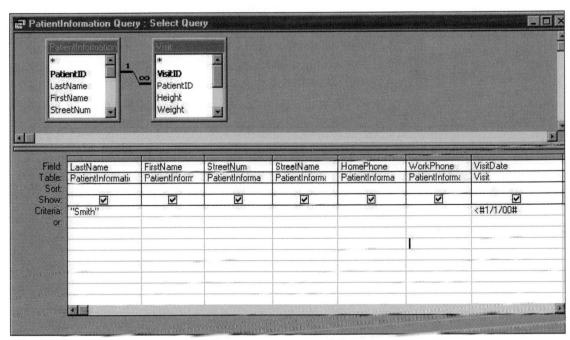

Figure 9.24

Query using information from two tables.

LastName	FirstName	StreetNum	...	WorkPhone	VisitDate
Adams	Jason	123	...	(703) 555-2345	03/19/99
Johnson	Linda	1002	...	(202) 555-9837	10/06/99
Smith	Mary	2340	...	(202) 555-4452	01/25/00
Adams	Jason	123	...	(703) 555-2345	12/20/99
Smith	Mary	2340	...	(202) 555-4452	11/25/99
Smith	George	3540	...	(301) 555-2347	01/22/00
Evans	Ellen	950	...	(703) 555-9596	12/01/99

Figure 9.25

Merged tables before criteria calculation.

LastName	FirstName	StreetNum	WorkPhone	VisitDate
Smith	Mary	2340	(202) 555-4452	11/25/99
Smith	George	3540	(301) 555-2347	12/19/99

Figure 9.26

Merged tables after criteria calculation.

Your Understanding

How is information retrieved effectively from a database?

temporary records, the records are compared with the criteria. If all the criteria are satisfied, the record is displayed; if *ANY* of the criteria are not satisfied, the record is not displayed.

The table in **Figure 9.26** shows the final result of the query from Figure 9.24. Only two records are displayed. Both records show the last name as Smith and both have a visit date before January 1, 2000.

Network Databases

Although desktop databases are useful for smaller organizations, most large companies use *network databases*. These databases can work almost exactly like a desktop database or can be accessed through the company's network or the Web. The biggest difference between a network database and a desktop database is that, with a network database, many different people may be looking at the information in the database at one time.

Because many people work with the same data, an attempt to change the data will sometimes fail. Two or more people cannot use or update the same data at the same time. The DBMS provides safeguards to eliminate the possibility of partial changes being made or having one set of changes cancel another.

One way of safeguarding the data is called *transactional processing.* The DBMS makes a choice and selects one of the changes to store in the database; the other changes are rejected. A transaction is a procedure that occurs as if it were a single operation.

To illustrate, let's assume that you are a sales representative entering a sale for construction material. A colleague who works in receiving is updating the prices because raw material costs increased this month. You enter the number of feet of lumber to sell and generate the bill at the same time your colleague is entering the new price for lumber. The system will either show you the new price, not generate the bill, and ask if you want to generate the bill again, or the system will wait until your transaction is completed before allowing the price of the lumber to be changed.

Another database function that can affect whether you can view or change data is called *record locking*. Record locking occurs whenever one user attempts to change the data in a record. The DBMS does not allow anyone else to access that record while the information is being changed. This procedure usually takes a short time and you probably won't notice any delay in receiving all the information into a form. Sometimes many records get locked, however, because someone is making a change to a large number of records or an entire table. In this case, your query gives you a blank form and the system shows you a message saying that the data is inaccessible. When this occurs, you must wait until the record is unlocked before requesting that record again.

Although transactional processing and record locking prevent errors from occurring because of simultaneous attempts to change the same record, they do not prevent users from entering incorrect data or data that cannot be queried properly. For this reason, you may be called on to create access and entry rules for large databases. Most of these rules are direct translations from the paper-record world, such as the proper formatting of names, addresses, and business names. Others may include specific abbreviations, such as for road types, part types, or names and other words used in your particular business. You may also be required to restrict access to some information.

Because databases with many users are usually enormous, checking every record is impossible. For this reason, properly designed procedures and thorough training are valuable tools in maintaining reliable records.

TERMS TO KNOW

1. Review these key terms and important terms.
   - alphanumeric
   - database
   - database management system (DBMS)
   - date
   - field
   - form
   - integer
   - key
   - link
   - logical
   - memo
   - network database
   - normalization
   - number
   - query
   - real
   - record
   - record locking
   - relational database
   - report
   - server
   - string
   - table
   - transactional processing
   - wizard

2. Select a term from the above list for each of these definitions.

   a. The database application that allows you to create and use a database?

   b. A field type that can hold up to 64K of text; used for adding comments to a record?

   c. A database with two or more tables that are related through one or more fields; this field must be a key field?

   d. A set of rules that allows selection of records from a database that meet specified criteria?

   e. A group of related records that all contain similar record design, in terms of field names and types?

   f. One category of information storage that cannot be broken down further; examples are name, date hired, part number?

   g. A field within a table whose value is unique within a table and is used to relate a record to one or more records in another table?

   h. A numeric value; a field that will be used in mathematical computations?

   i. A field type that will contain a date or time?

   j. A field type that refers (or links) to an external, usually large, field?

3. Select 10 terms from the list of key terms and important terms that were not used in Item 2. Define these terms in your own words.

DISCUSSION QUESTIONS

Answer each question as a written assignment or for class discussion. Be concise in your responses.

1. Explain what a field is and give some examples of fields that can be included in an Inventory table.

2. Define *record*.

3. Define *table*.

4. Give one reason why you might store a zip code as a string and not a number.

5. Explain the purpose of a form.

6. What type of field would you use to store the beginning time of a work shift?

7. Name four parts of a modern DBMS.

8. What would you need to design if you wanted to examine all customers living in 202 area code, provided the database with customer information already exists?

CRITICAL THINKING

1. **Gather Facts**   From the classified advertising section of a local or national newspaper, find and list the major headings or classifications of the advertisements. Three examples of major heads are Legal Notices, Employment, and Real Estate.

2. **Generalize from Facts**   Write a statement that addresses this question: How might an electronic database be used by the editors of the newspaper to make the placement and display of classified advertisements efficient and orderly?

3. **Create New Ideas**   Suggest fields and tables that might be used for a classified advertisement database. Name an example of a record that might appear in one or more tables.

NETWORKING WITH THE REAL WORLD

Access *Embark.com: Scholarship Search*. The address is http://embark.com/faid.asp. Determine if you might qualify for a scholarship, and report your findings orally or in writing.

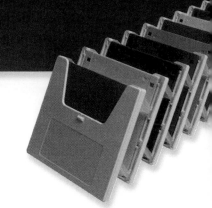

Network-Based Records Management

The purpose of Chapter 10 is to enable you to:

- Identify the major components of a computer network.
- Describe the functions of servers, clients, and peers in a computer network.
- Cite how to make files and directories available to other computers.
- Explain how to access and modify files on another computer.
- Describe how to enter information into electronic records using proper records management techniques.

KEY TERMS

- **access rights**
- **address**
- **file server**
- **Internet**
- **intranet**
- **Lan (local area network)**
- **network**
- **path**
- **protocol**
- **remote access**
- **TLD**
- **World Wide Web**

The introduction of computer networks into the workplace has added a new level of challenges for the Records management professional. Instead of printing electronic records to paper, or copying files to a disk for transfer from one computer to another, individuals can access or send electronic records quickly and easily. This presents another level of complexity in the management of records in an organization. How do you enforce filing and naming rules? How is the transfer of records from one company to another achieved? What is now considered reference material? All of these questions are affected by the introduction of electronic computer networks within the workplace. In this chapter we will discuss how computer networks work, what the advantages and pitfalls are, and how a Records management professional can track and control electronic records within a large organization. We will also discuss how the Internet has affected the management of information both inside and outside the organization.

Computer Networks

In Chapters 8 and 9, electronic information management was considered largely from the standpoint of a single computer. Only a few years ago, a typical method of moving information from one computer to another was to save files on floppy disks and physically take them to another computer. Although other means of moving files from one computer to another have existed for many years, it took the onset of the Internet and the World Wide Web to bring computer networks and the electronic transfer of information into the majority of national and international workplaces.

A computer **network** is a set of cables and equipment designed to connect computers electronically, like a road network connects cities to one another. The cables, electronic boxes, and a special set of rules for communicating allow each computer to access other computers that are connected to the network so they can communicate with one another. Computer networks let us share information easily with others. There are three ways information can be shared electronically:

1. A document can be sent to another computer.
2. Documents on each individual computer can be made available to others for access.
3. Documents can be stored on a central computer and accessed by all authorized users.

In this chapter we will concentrate on defining networks and describing how to use a network-based records management system. We will also discuss some of the unique challenges of gathering information from the Internet.

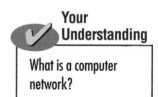

Your Understanding

What is a computer network?

Computer Network Basics

A network is a means for one computer to communicate with another. The earliest computer network was simply a cable connected between two computers. Each computer would use a program that "pretended" to be a disk drive. Each computer could read information from that program and treat it as another hardware component.

In the late 1960s, researchers began to devise schemes to allow several computers to share a cable and communicate with any other computer attached to that cable. To accomplish this procedure, each computer needed a unique identifier or **address.** Each computer also had to use the same rules and procedures to share the cable.

Several types of computer networks are in use today. Although they are not always able to communicate with one another, each network type has a few features in common:

- A way for each computer to be identified uniquely.
- A way for each computer to contact every other computer on the network.
- A way for one computer to send a message, file, or command to another.

A network consists of four components:

1. The computers that use the network. These computers have two basic functions: to request information from and to send information to another computer.
2. The wires, fiber-optic cable, or radio waves that carry the information. These items are called the *network media.*
3. A special set of rules that allow one computer to send information to and receive information from another. The set of rules that allows the computers to find one another and begin a conversation is called a **protocol.**
4. Electronics that exist in the network for the sole purpose of sending a message from one computer to another. This *network equipment* consists of specialized computers and computer components that translate the signals into useful information (see **Figure 10.1**).

Computer Network Components

- Computers
- Network media
- Protocol
- Network equipment

Communication Between Computers

Computers communicate with each other using a protocol, or a set of rules for establishing communication. It is called a protocol because it works the same way diplomats do when they greet each other. One diplomat will utter a greeting, the second will reply, the first will extend a hand to shake, and the second will respond in kind. Once that process is complete, the two can sit and begin to discuss the issue at hand. A

Your Understanding

What are the four components of networks?

Figure 10.1

Inside a network room. *In what ways can this environment be protected or secured?*

networked computer follows a similar procedure to create a communications link with another computer:

- Computer 1 sends a request for communication with computer 2 onto the network.
- Computer 2 sees a message addressed to it and reads it. It then replies to computer 1 (which included its address in its message) and says that it may have a conversation.
- Computer 1 sends an affirmative response to computer 2, and a communication is established. At this point, computer 1 starts sending information, such as a document, to computer 2.
- When computer 1 is finished, it sends a message that says it has completed its communication.
- Computer 2 responds that it understands and stops the communication at its end.

- Computer 1 also stops "talking." The communication has ended.

There can be different protocols for different activities, such as printing and e-mail. Activities can take place on the same physical network because the computers will ignore any requests that they do not understand.

How Network Computers Function

Network Computer Functions

- Client
- Server
- Peer

When computers communicate with one another, they function as either a client, a server, or a peer. A *client* is a computer that is requesting information. When you "surf" the Web, your computer is functioning as a client. Clients request information from servers.

A *server* is a computer that is serving other computers, or giving them information. Servers do not usually have people sitting at their keyboards working. Their job is to store files and wait for a request from a client.

Computers functioning as *peers* both request and give information; they have equivalent jobs. A good example of peer communication is a videoconferencing session. When you sit in front of your screen, you can see the other person or people on other computers because your computer requests their images from their computer. They, in turn, can see you because your computer sends them your image.

Local Area Networks (LANs)

At work, most employees communicate with other employees in the same business or organization. A network that connects the computers within a business is called a **local area network (LAN).** For communications to operate effectively, all the computers on the LAN must have the same protocols.

Some offices may have both Macintoshes (Macs) and personal computers (PCs) connected to the same network. They can communicate with each other as long as they use the same protocol. It is easier to move a file from a Mac to a PC over a network, than to use a floppy disk, which would require conversion programs.

Once connected to a network using the proper protocol, a computer must be able to identify the other computers on the network and be able to send messages so that the other

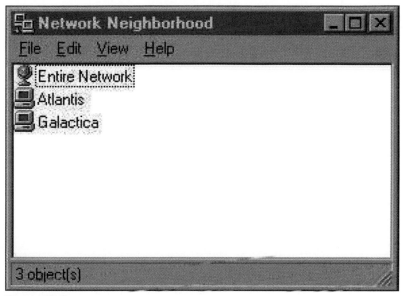

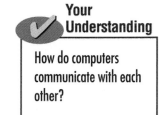

Figure 10.2

Network Neighborhood. *Once connected to a network using proper protocol, what must a computer be able to identify on the network?*

computers can reply. To perform these tasks, each computer has a unique address. This address can be a number or a name. The addresses are assigned by the company's network administrator, who is a specialist in setting up and maintaining networks.

When you double-click on the Network Neighborhood icon on your Microsoft Windows desktop, you can see which computers are available. You will also see any printers that are connected directly to the network. **Figure 10.2** shows an example of a network neighborhood.

The Internet

Within a company, computers can be connected to a LAN fairly easily. The network administrator has the authority to decide what protocols and what network cable type to use. But other companies could be using different protocols and different network types. How do they communicate with one another? This situation is where the Internet is useful. **Internet** means a network of networks. The Internet allows a computer to exchange information with other computers all over the world. A company's network can talk to another company's network using a special protocol called TCP/IP. This protocol has been in use since the 1970s and is the recognized standard for connecting large networks. Another point about the Internet is that there is only one. Many companies own parts of it, but every computer that uses the Internet can get a message to or from any other computer on the Internet.

Domain Names

In the discussion of LANs, you learned that addresses or identifiers for each computer are required. These addresses or identifiers are important for the Internet, but with a significant difference. Computer names on the Internet have parts. Your home address has a street, a city, and a state. The computer's address has a computer name, a company or organization name, and a category name. All these parts form the *domain name.* If you have used a software application to locate and display documents on the Web, (called a Web browser), you have seen the familiar www.mycompany.com. Because "mycompany" is a for-profit entity, it is given the "com" organization category. This last part of the domain name (com) is called a **top-level domain (TLD).**

All organizations using the Internet have domains. Most of these top-level domain names consist of a three-character abbreviation that identifies the type of organization. Sample domain names and an explanation of the six three-letter TLD organizational categories are shown in **Figure 10.3.**

Domains can also describe geographic location. These domains have a two-letter TLD (instead of three). These TLD codes are called *country codes.* Some examples of geographic-based domain names are shown in **Figures 10.4** and **10.5.**

E-Mail

By far, the service used most often on the Internet is electronic mail, or *e-mail.* E-mail allows people to communicate with one another in writing or graphics with the convenience and immediacy of a telephone but without the need for the recipient to be available when the message is sent. Thus, e-mail has advantages of both the telephone and postal mail.

Domain Name	Name and Description of TLD
www.nasa.gov	***National Aeronautics and Space Administration*** **.gov** means that the organization is part of the United States government other than the military.
www.af.mil	***United States Air Force*** **.mil** means that the organization is part of the United States military.
www.vt.edu	***Virginia Tech*** **.edu** is used for four year institutions (colleges and universities) in the United States.
www.earthlink.net	*EarthLink* (an Internet service provider) **.net** is used for organizations that are gathering places for other organizations or people. Internet service providers, programmer groups, family groups, and company joint ventures are among the organizations that use the .netTLD.
www.unitedway.org	***United Way*** **.org** is used by any nonprofit organizations and educational organizations that do not qualify for .edu (such as private, technical, and vocational schools).
www.ibm.com	***IBM*** **.com** is used by for-profit organizations. Companies, whether or not they sell products on the Internet, have a .com TLD.

Note 1: Although .edu, .mil, and .gov require that the organization be based in the United States, the other TLDs do not.

Note 2: The www at the beginning of each name indicates that the machine being addressed is a Web server. The www is not required for a Web server, it is simply a popular convention.

Figure 10.3

Domain names. ***What domain name would you give to the Kodak Corporation's website?***

Domain Name	Name and Description of TLD
www.state.va.us	*Commonwealth of Virginia* **.us** is United States (all state Web sites look like www.state.xx.us) where xx is the U.S. Postal Service two-letter state abbreviation.
www.cam.ac.uk	*Cambridge University, Cambridge England* **.uk** is United Kingdom (England). In England .ac.uk ends a university domain name, and .co.uk ends a company domain name. (Other countries have naming schemes similar to England's.)

Figure 10.4

Domain names with country codes. *What would be the complete domain name for Ohio's web site?*

TLD	Country Name
de	Germany
jp	Japan
ca	Canada
mx	Mexico
it	Italy
se	Sweden
kr	South Korea

Figure 10.5

A sample of other country TLDs. *What would be the TLD for France?*

E-mail has its disadvantages, however. A disadvantage that affects the job of a records management professional is that the ease of e-mail transmission means that many trivial messages as well as important ones are sent. Many people feel overwhelmed by the amount of e-mail they receive; 200 messages a day is not uncommon. Another disadvantage is that senders often do not choose their words in an e-mail message as carefully as they do in written letters or telephone conversations. Such carelessness can result in miscommunication, anger, and even legal action being taken against the sender of an e-mail message.

When sending an e-mail message on a local area network, you can usually address it to the person by using his or her first and last names. If there are two or more persons with the same name, the e-mail application will open a window asking you to select the correct person.

On the Internet, every person who can receive e-mail must have a unique address. All e-mail addresses are in the form e-mailname@domainname (Jason.smith@mycompany.com or jsmith@mycompany.com). The "@" symbol separates the person's e-mail name from the domain name.

The standard form of an e-mail address cannot have spaces or special characters except an underscore or a period. However, not all internet service providers (ISP) require that an e-mail address follow standard form. E-mail names that do not follow standard form may have difficulty being transmitted. Therefore, to guarantee delivery and receipt of e-mail messages, choose an e-mail address that follows standard form. You can ask your ISP for Internet format standards as well as request a guarantee that your e-mail address will work anywhere on the Internet. An ISP will not make such a guarantee if your e-mail address does not follow standard form.

The World Wide Web

Another important part of the Internet is called the **World Wide Web,** or the **Web.** People often equate the Web and the Internet, although they are really two different entities. The Internet consists of computers all over the world that carry data and allow the exchange of information. The Web is a subset of the Internet. It is a collection of documents linked together using an Internet protocol called *http,* or *hypertext transfer protocol.* Web browsers communicate with a server using http to retrieve text, images, and sound documents and put them together. The Web allows users to move easily from one document to another document on the Internet because the addresses of documents are embedded in other documents.

We have already discussed the computer's address as having a domain name such as www.mycompany.com. In a Web address, the computer name is followed by extra information that refers to the document you wish to view. The protocol, the computer's domain name, and the document information is called the *uniform resource locator (URL)*. A URL is a means of addressing any document available on the Internet.

Figure 10.6 shows a URL and all its components. The first part, called the *method,* is the protocol used for communication with the server, as discussed on page 156. The Internet uses TCP/IP to set up a connection between the computers. After the connection is established, the programs must still communicate with each other. Each program (or set of programs) can use its own protocol in addition to the protocol used to set up the connection between the computers.

Everything after the method is called the **path,** which is a combination of the domain name, the folder names, and a file name that defines the address. You must follow this path to reach the document you want. First, you must find the computer, then the correct folder, and last the file. The three components of the path are described in more detail in the following:

- The first component is the domain name, such as www.companyname.TLD (organizational type [com, edu, org, net, gov] or two-letter country code).
- The domain name is followed by a slash (/) then the *relative path.* The relative path is the list of the folders you must go through to get to the document on the computer containing that document.
- Last is the actual document name. On the Web, most document names are followed by *.html.* Although

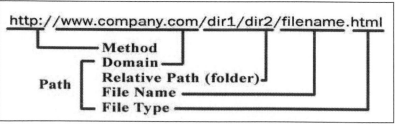

Figure 10.6

Basic URL structure. ***Can you recognize the domain name and its parts?***

URL Components

- Method
- Path
- Domain
- Relative path
- Document name
- File type

technically it is not required, a file type is still used for nearly all Web-based documents.

The Web has some unique advantages over other ways of accessing computers on the Internet. The foremost advantage is its ability to allow one electronic record to reference another through a mechanism called a *hyperlink*. Hyperlinks allow a document to include the address of another document so that when a person selects certain blocks or bits of text or pictures, the new document is retrieved.

Your Understanding

What is the difference between the internet and the World Wide Web?

Network File Systems

Within a local area network, there are two ways to store electronic records: distributed on individual desktop computers, and in a central location.

Distributed Storage of Electronic Records

Within small companies, electronic records are stored on desktop computers, and the LAN is used for e-mail, printing, and access to the Internet. This arrangement is also typical for companies in the process of transition from a paper-based records system to an electronic one.

Initially, when a computer joins a LAN, it can view other computers and documents, but no one else can view its documents. However, you can allow other computers on the LAN to see folders on your computer through a process called *sharing* (see **Figure 10.7**). You can select the folders you wish to share. For example, if you share the "Sales" folder within your "California" folder, people on other computers can access the "Sales" folder, but they will not be able to see or access the "California" folder. Because the share name they see is "Sales," you would probably want to change it to "California Sales" or "CA Sales" to make it more descriptive. You can also set a password so only authorized users can have access to the folders you share, or you can set permissions for individuals or groups.

Once you have turned on sharing for a folder, other people on the network will be able to see that folder and any files

Figure 10.7

Windows 95 sharing
property.

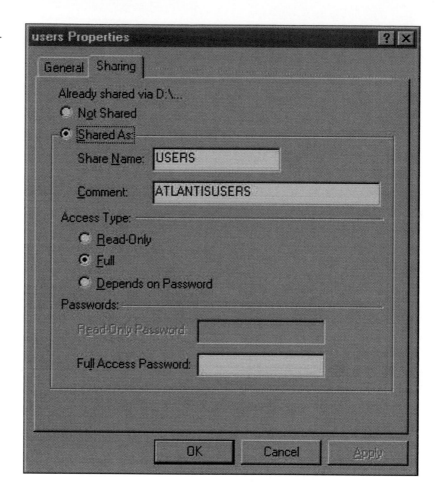

and folders contained in it. When someone from a different
computer accesses your machine, they see only shared folders
and printers. In **Figure 10.8,** a person has accessed a folder
called "HandheldPC," which is a subfolder in the "Software"
share on the computer called "Galactica." The share called
"Software" might be a folder by a different name or it might be
a hard drive. To people on other computers, folders and drives
look the same.

RECORDS MANAGEMENT OF DISTRIBUTED FILES When files
are located on multiple computers, the management of these
files becomes difficult. Certain policies can be implemented to
manage shared files:

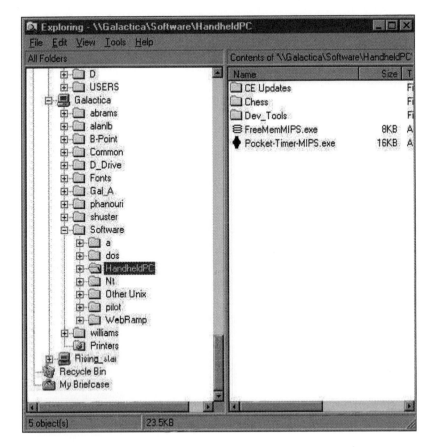

Figure 10.8

Shared folder on the LAN.
*What do you think would
be some benefits for
sharing a folder?*

- Provide all workers with written procedures for creating
  file names, folder names, and metadata. Procedures
  should stipulate conditions under which the file can be
  moved, destroyed, or recycled.

- Define what constitutes a company record (see Chapter 1)
  and require that folders containing these files be shared.
  The system administrator should have full right to view
  and edit all files.

- Use a backup system capable of saving files from the
  network and set up backup procedures for all shared
  resources throughout the LAN.

- Set up a procedure for moving files to another machine or
  to a central location when an employee leaves the
  company or moves to another department.

Central Storage of Electronic Records

Another option for storing electronic records is to store them all on the same computer. This type of computer is called a **file server** and is designed solely to manage computer files for other computers. A file server is not meant to be used for everyday work but rather to store huge numbers of electronic records for the company or organization.

Using a central storage method allows a records management professional to:

- Ensure that there is a definitive version of a particular document because only one copy of the document will be accessed and updated by everyone on the LAN.

- Control access to electronic records through the use of file permissions.

- Track who accesses electronic records by creating a log on the file server. The log will show the date and the time when the records were accessed, and which computer accessed the records.

- Protect records by backing up the file server regularly, thereby ensuring that important records are not vulnerable.

To access stored records, a user must have permission. Also, the software application required to open the record must exist on the computer being used. Access to the document can be achieved in one of two ways. The first is similar to accessing a shared document on a desktop computer, which we discussed in "Distributed Storage of Electronic Records" on page 163. The second way is to give your computer the impression that it has another hard drive, which is actually the file server. This procedure is done by creating a *mapped drive.* On the server, a share is created as discussed in "Distributed Storage of Electronic Records." The difference is that the client computers use the drive mapping tool in Windows to connect the share to a drive letter, instead of using the Network Neighborhood icon (see **Figure 10.9**). Another feature of a mapped drive is that it is connected automatically to the file server every time a computer user logs on.

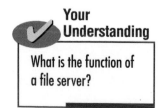

Your Understanding

What is the function of a file server?

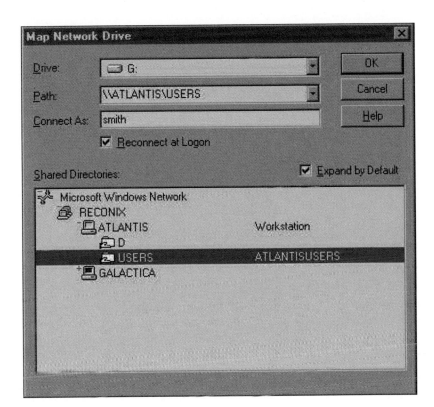

Figure 10.9

Setting up a mapped drive.
How do you think the term "file server" relates to what it does?

Naming Conventions

A records manager for a central file system must be concerned with the naming rules on all computers that have access to the file server. The names of folders and files must be compatible with all computers accessing them. UNIX machines, for example, do not allow spaces in file names. If there are computers running DOS or versions of Microsoft Windows before Windows 95, then the file name cannot be longer than eight characters and cannot have any special characters except an underscore (_).

When computers using DOS or Windows 3.x operating systems use the network, files will be accessible if they have more than eight characters in the name, but they will be reduced to the first five or six characters plus an index code. For example, ConventionSales.doc might look like CONVEN ~ 1.DOC on a Windows 3.11 computer.

Instead of . . .	New File Name	DOS Name
Letter.George L Smith.30Jan1999	GLS30Jan99Ltr	GLS30J ~ 2
Northwest Region Sales Jan–Jun	NWSales_JanJun	NWSALE ~ 1

Figure 10.10

Renaming files for compatibility with older computers. *How would you rename Maintenance Procedures.Printing Press.30July2000?*

If these older computers are part of your network, then you should make the first six characters of the file name the most specific. **Figure 10.10** lists two examples. The endings on the DOS file names (~ 1, ~ 2, etc.) are required to make the file name unique within the folder. The endings begin with ~ 1 and increase based on the date that the file is created. In the second entry in Figure 10.10, if you create the July through December Sales document for the Northwest Region, the new file would be called NWSales_JulDec for most people and NWSAL ~ 2 for DOS users.

If the number of files with the same first part of the file name increases beyond five, then you should create a separate folder for those files. **Figure 10.11** shows examples.

When computers using DOS or Windows 3.x are not part of the organization, long file names are generally acceptable. There are still significant restrictions, however, on the characters allowed in a file name. The most significant restriction is that spaces are not allowed by UNIX and mainframe computers. You need to examine the file naming rules for each of the computer systems used on your network and devise naming schemes accordingly.

Several methods are available for reducing the need for spaces and other special characters (see **Figure 10.12**):

- Use an underscore (_) or a dot (.) in place of spaces.
- Begin each word or abbreviation with an uppercase letter and make the other characters lowercase where possible.
- Substitute a hyphen (–) for other special characters such as \ , /, +, ( ), [ ], and { }.

Old File Name	New Folder	New File Name*
Letter.George Smith.30Jan2003	Smith_G	Ltr_30Jan2003
Fax.George Smith.20Feb2003		Fax_20Feb2003
Quote.George Smith.15Mar2003		Qte_15Mar2003
Northwest Region Sales Jan-Jun02	NWSales	02JanJun
Northwest Region Sales Jul-Dec02		02JulDec
Northwest Region Sales Jan-Jun03		03JanJun
Northwest Region Sales Jan-Jun02		02JulDec

*Dates in file names can be coded several different ways. Once a dating scheme is devised, it should be implemented for all files and folder names within the file server.

Figure 10.11

Establishing separate folders. *What folder names might you assign for memos from Brian Mackin regarding new procedures?*

Instead of . . .	New File Name
Letter.George Smith.30Jan2003	SmithGeorge.30Jan03.ltr
Northwest Region Sales Jan-Jun	NW_Sales_Jan-Jun
Proposal for Highway 655 (Initial)	Hwy655.Proposal-Init-

Figure 10.12

Minimizing file names. *What other ways can you think of to minimize the original file names?*

- Eliminate common words where possible.
- Although not usually required, brevity is still desirable.

Access Rights (File Servers)

SECURITY Because every computer connected to the entire LAN will have access to the file server, you may want to prevent certain people from accessing some of the files. For example, payroll information should not be visible to anyone outside that department. Other documents, especially those no longer being modified, must be protected from accidental erasure or modification. All these concerns are addressed by **access rights** settings on the file server.

Creating a share on a file server also gives you the ability to set access rights, or permissions, based on the type of user (which is set when the username is created), or on individual users. File permissions allow the following types of access:

- **None:** The user or group of users does not have permission to view the file, copy it, or edit it.

- **Read:** The user or group of users may view the file or make a copy to their desktop computer, but they may not modify the file-server version of the file.

- **Change:** The user or group of users may read, copy, or make changes to the file, but they cannot delete it.

- **Full:** The user or group of users may read, copy, change, or delete the file.

Types of Access Rights

- None
- Read
- Change
- Full

NAMING   If you have a sales department, an accounting department, a personnel group, and an engineering group in your organization, you can define a share for each group on the shared folder. All the workers in the group will have the same permissions. Assign a name to each share (see **Figure 10.13**). If you have DOS or earlier Windows computers using the LAN, you must use a share name of eight characters or fewer.

If many older computers are part of the network, it is preferable to increase the number of folders so that more information can be provided with readable file names.

Intranets

Another popular means of distributing electronic records is to build an organizational version of the World Wide Web. That is, create Web documents that are available only to people using the company's LAN, not the Internet in general. Such a network is called an **intranet** instead of Internet because it is available only within the borders of the company or organization; however, it uses the rules of the Internet for access. An intranet has certain advantages:

Department	Possible DOS Share Name
Accounting	Acct
Personnel	Persnl
Sales	Sales
Engineering	Eng

Figure 10.13

Assigning names in a share. *What other share names can you think of for the original names?*

- It has all the capability of the Internet: hyperlinks, ease of use, and universal ability to view documents using Web browsers.

- It is accessible from outside the LAN with a proper username and password, without the need for special equipment.

- It is easier to build multiple filing systems with the same set of records using Web pages that act as the file browser used on a desktop computer. Today, applications that connect to the Web server allow you to design filing systems that are based, for example, on topic, geography, date, and customer. Any new document added to the intranet using this system would appear automatically in all of the filing systems in the appropriate folder.

Remote File Access

Sometimes you will have to access a document when you are away from your office. The office LAN can be accessed temporarily through a process called *remote log-in*. This process allows you to access one computer from another as if you were in your office. Most office users will either connect directly with their desktop computer or use a modem to connect to a server that allows access to the LAN.

CONSOLE EMULATION A popular method for home computer users and small organizations is to run an application

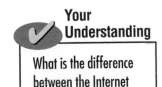

Your Understanding

What is the difference between the Internet and intranet?

called a *console emulation* program. This program allows a person from a remote screen to take over the functions of another computer's monitor, keyboard, and mouse. The person at the remote screen can access the office computer through a modem or over the Internet. A popular version of this type of program is Symantec PC Anywhere. The drawback is that the application must be installed at both the office computer and the remote computer. Many people who use this console emulation have an office computer and a laptop for computer use away from the office.

REMOTE ACCESS SERVICE   Another method of access is called *remote access service* or *RAS*. This method allows the remote computer to access the LAN using a modem or the Internet. A server computer or a special piece of network equipment allows the remote computer to act as another computer on the LAN, even though it is not physically within the local network. This method is preferred by larger organizations and companies because users have access to the network with the same permissions and restrictions that they have at the office but without the necessity of adding expensive software to every computer in the company.

Locating Networked Information

In larger organizations, even diligent naming schemes and supervision may not be enough to make finding a document simple. Several tools are available to help find documents. On a LAN, the Find tool and the advanced search option discussed in Chapter 8 work as well on a file server as on a desktop computer. On the Internet, however, you don't have the ability to search for files. Instead, you search for concepts and keywords. For example, if you want to obtain information about software applications providing document management solutions, you can use the keywords "document management."

Search Engines

Because the Internet has millions of documents organized in several ways, searching for information using systematic methods is practically impossible. Applications called *search engines* have been developed to help manage the search for information on the Internet. The vast majority of searchable documents are Web pages. Because Web pages are connected to one another with hyperlinks, a search engine can find new documents automatically.

The job of a search engine is to collect information. To collect information, it goes from Web site to Web site, downloading pages (receiving files from the network) automatically, as if it were a person browsing the site. It then finds every hyperlink in the document and gets the pages found at those links. Once it has collected the Web pages, it creates a list for the site based on words within the document. Some search engines use only keywords or the title of the document, while others use every word in the document to create a catalog of the information. The address and cataloged information are stored in a database.

When you search using one or several keywords, all documents containing that keyword are retrieved from the database. A ranking is created based on the number of times the keyword appears in each document and how it is used. The search engine then displays a list of documents containing the keyword, with the highest ranking documents at the top of the list. Because search engines use different methods to create the ranking and because many Web sites are not searched, a particular document may be at the top of the ranking list for a search using one engine, but not listed at all when using another. While all search engines allow simple searches (a list of words to look for), some will let you ask a question (a *natural language search*) or create a complex search by selecting elements such as words or phrases, words to exclude, or document age. **Figure 10.14** lists some World Wide Web search engines and their capabilities.

> **Search Engines**
>
> Help to search for information on the Internet.

Search Engines			
Name	**URL**	**Advanced Search?**	**Natural Language?**
AltaVista	http://www.altavista.com	Yes	Partially
Excite	http://www.excite.com	Yes	No
Goto	http://www.goto.com	Yes, but no help	Yes
HotBot	http://www.hotbot.com	Yes (many settings)	No
Infoseek	http://infoseek.go.com	Yes	No
InfoSpace	http://www.infospace.com	No	No
Yahoo	http://www.yahoo.com	Yes	Partially

Figure 10.14

Search engines. *What part of each URL is the domain name?*

Network Directories

An alternative to automated search engines is the use of directories. Directories are a listing of Web sites organized by topic. The topics (such as recreation, health, and travel) are developed by the staff of the company hosting the directory service. These topics are updated with new Web site addresses by the staff of the directory service or by individuals when they submit their Web sites. The best known of these directory services is Yahoo. When using a Web directory, the sites you find are usually more relevant than those found by a search engine, but the site must be one of the topic areas defined by the directory service. Of the search engines listed in **Figure 10.14,** AltaVista, InfoSpace, and Yahoo also provide directories in addition to the search engine.

Software Agents

Because there are so many different search engines and directories on the Internet, other applications, *software agents* or *metasearch* engines, have been devised to help search the Internet more thoroughly. These applications take your words and phrases, request a Web search from five or more search engines, and collate and return the results to you. The best known metasearch site is called AskJeeves. This software agent takes a natural language question and builds the search words and phrases based on that question. It then sends a query to many search engines using words, phrases, and logical or boolean search questions to obtain the most accurate results. Other metasearch agents are Northernlights, Dogpile, and Apple Computer's Sherlock.

Self-Describing Documents

Another increasingly popular method of categorizing information on the Internet embeds values in the document that describe what each word or phrase means. It is similar to creating the metadata discussed in Chapter 8, but it can be attributed to individual words, phrases, and other parts of an electronic record rather than to the record as a whole. This use of descriptive information within the document allows it to be *self-describing*, which means that you can select a word or phrase and know that it is, for example, the title of the paragraph, or select a number and see that it is the weight of an inventory item.

The technology used to implement self-description is called *XML* or *extensible markup language*. This feature allows special markers, called *tags*, to be placed in the document that tell the application what the words within the tags mean or how they are to be displayed. XML is similar to html, the language of the Web, but it is much more powerful. Because the tags themselves can be defined, a different set of XML tags can be developed for different organizations. These tags can be used to refine your Web search. For example, if you use a search engine to search on "chip," you will be given a list of documents that contain that word. Some of the documents will reference computer chips and others will reference potato chips. XML allows you to search on "chip" and state that you are interested in food. Records management professionals may be creating these XML descriptions as part of their future duties.

TERMS TO KNOW

1. Review these key terms and important terms.

- access rights
- address
- console emulation
- country code
- client
- domain name
- e-mail
- file server
- html
- http
- hyperlink
- Internet
- intranet
- LAN (local area network)
- mapped drive
- metasearch
- method
- natural language search
- network
- network equipment
- network media
- path
- peer
- protocol
- RAS (remote access service)
- relative path
- remote access
- remote log-in
- search engine
- self-describing
- server
- sharing
- software agents
- tag
- TLD (top level domain)
- URL (uniform resource locator)
- World Wide Web
- XML (extensible markup language)

2. Write one or two paragraphs that contain each key term. Underline or italicize each term.

DISCUSSION QUESTIONS

Answer each question as a written assignment or for class discussion. Be concise in your responses.

1. What are the differences between a client computer and a server computer?

2. What is a peer computer?

3. Explain the importance of a protocol.

4. What is a LAN?

5. What might the URL be for the web site of a company called Fulton Motors?

6. List at least three reasons for storing electronic records on a central file server.

7. What is the difference between a metasearch and a regular search?

CRITICAL THINKING

1. **Gather Facts** Select a topic that is of interest to you and is related to this or another class. Use the Internet to research the topic. Prepare a written report.

2. **Generalize from Facts** In writing, discuss the advantages and disadvantages of using the Internet versus the library to research a topic.

3. **Create New Ideas** Develop a guideline for Internet researchers that include specific steps for obtaining information about a subject.

NETWORKING WITH THE REAL WORLD

Form a group of four to eight students in your computer lab. As a group, create a shared folder with access permissions for about half of the group (or give the share a password). Have each member of the group attempt to retrieve a document from another computer using the newly created share.

COMPUTER APPLICATIONS

Complete each of the following tasks in lab or on your home computer. Be prepared to discuss what you did in class.

1. Create a small document and save it in a directory that is not at the root of the hard drive. Share the folder that the document is saved in and have someone else retrieve it and make changes. You can create a shared folder from Windows Explorer as follows:

   - Select the folder you wish to make available to others.

   - Right-click on the Folder icon and select "Properties." (If your computer is set up properly, you should see a tab called Sharing.)

   - Select the Sharing tab to tell the computer to share the folder. A name will be created. You can change the name to something descriptive.

2. Select a topic that requires Internet research. Use regular searches (with a list of words), advanced searches (using dates and phrases, and a boolean search), and natural language searches (with AskJeeves or Goto). Compare the results of these searches in terms of the number of items returned and their relevance to the actual search topic.

Image Technology and Automated Systems

The purpose of Chapter 11 is to enable you to:

- Classify the major elements of any image technology system.
- Define terms related to image technology and automated systems.
- Categorize techniques and equipment associated with each technology.
- Clarify how each technology increases efficiency in records and information management.
- Describe types of automated records management systems used to monitor an organization's records.
- Identify three major considerations in selecting an automated records management system.
- Discuss issues to be addressed by the records and information manager for each of the three major considerations identified.

KEY TERMS

- automated records management system
- bar code
- CD-R
- CD-RW
- computer generated output
- data image
- DVD
- GUI
- ICR
- image technology

- keyword search
- menu-driven
- MICR
- microfiche
- microfilm
- OCR
- OMR
- reader or viewer
- real image
- wildcard search

Many business and government organizations must handle large quantities of data. To reduce the increasing expense of storing and retrieving paper records, organizations are taking advantage of image technology. **Image technology** refers to the conversion of paper records to photographic or electronic form and the administration of the new form.

Image Technology

Regardless of the specific hardware and software used in image technology, there are four major elements in any image technology system:

- *Input,* or *capture,* refers to converting paper records to electronic form.

- *Indexing* is assigning to each electronic document image a unique, logical identifier or identifiers. For example, in a bank checking account file, each account can be indexed by one or more of the following: account number, social security number, and/or name.

- *Storing* is directing the system to send images to a location where they can be saved until needed.

- *Retrieving* is directing the system to obtain images from storage so they can be read, printed, or manipulated.

An image may be an exact representation of a paper record, in which case it is called a **real image.** An example of a real image is the picture of a check that a bank might create. The image may also be certain information captured from a paper record, called a **data image.** An example of a data image is the information taken by a grocery store scanner from the bar code on a box of cereal.

There are two major kinds of real images: filmed images and scanned images. Filmed images are miniature photographs of paper records; scanned images are representations of paper records in computer memory.

Image Technology

The conversion of paper records In photographic or electronic form.

Your Understanding

What are the major elements of an image technology system?

Types of Real Images

- Filmed images
- Scanned images

Real Images—Filmed

Micrographic Technology

- Film:
  - microfilm
  - microfiche
- Equipment:
  - microfilmer
    - reader/viewer
    - reader/printer

The traditional means of capturing real images has been the use of special cameras, called *microfilmers,* to take miniature, or micrographic, pictures of paper records **(Figure 11.1)**. The pictures can be in rolls, called **microfilm (Figure 11.2)**, or on flat, transparent film sheets, called **microfiche (Figure 11.3)**. A microfilm roll can contain hundreds of document images on either 16-mm, 35-mm, or 105-mm film. A 4-by-6-inch microfiche sheet can also store hundreds of document images. Each document on microfilm or microfiche is a *microform* or *microrecord.*

To look at a document that has been microfilmed, you must use a machine called a **reader** or **viewer.** These machines magnify the miniature images and display them on a screen. A *reader/printer* displays images on a screen and can also print full-size documents on paper **(Figure 11.4).**

Figure 11.1

Microfilm camera.

Figure 11.2

Roll of microfilm. *What type of information do you think could be stored on microfilm or microfiche?*

Figure 11.3

Microfiche.

Figure 11.4

Reader/printer. *What is it that the reader does to the microfilm or microfiche?*

Advantages of Microforms

- Low cost of storage
- Durability
- Low shipment cost
- Fast retrieval

Micrographic technology greatly reduces the cost of storage space. For example, a single 4-by-6-inch sheet of microfiche can hold the same amount of information as a box of 100 paper documents. A single roll of microfilm can hold the same amount of information as several boxes containing hundreds of documents. By reducing the documents to micro size, the amount of space needed to store the documents is greatly reduced. Microforms also have the advantage of durability, low shipment cost, and fast retrieval.

Real Images—Scanned

A newer way to capture real images is to use an image scanner to read documents and convert them to computer memory. An *image scanner* is a machine into which paper documents are fed for conversion to electronic form, usually onto one of several types of disks. Another name for an image scanner is *high speed image camera.* The technology of using image scanners to convert an image of text into computer-editable text is known as **optical character recognition (OCR).**

The use of computer disks to store real images is referred to as *disk technology.* Disks are used as input to a computer system or database to manage the scanned documents. Compared with microform technology, disk technology has the potential for even greater savings of time, money, and space. A 1 gigabyte disk can store as much information as 1 million pages of paper documents. Several of the most popular disks are:

- **Compact disk recordable (CD-R):** This disk is a relatively inexpensive medium. Data can be recorded onto it only once **(Figure 11.5).**

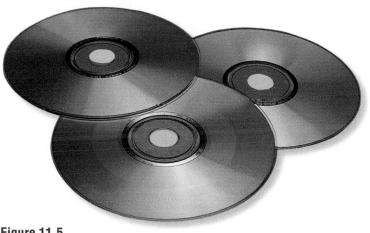

Figure 11.5

Compact disks (CDs). *How are you most familiar with CDs?*

Disk Technology

- CD-R
- CD-RW
- DVD
- Hard disk
- Redundant array

Your Understanding

What are the two types of real images?

- **Compact disk-rewritable (CD-RW):** This disk is a more expensive medium, but new data can be recorded over old data. It is often used for backup, but it is not suitable for very important data, sometimes referred to as archive data.

- **Digital video [or versitale] disk (DVD):** An emerging technology that some experts say will supplement, or even replace, compact disk technology.

- **Hard disk:** With the availability of inexpensive, large-capacity hard drives, it is no longer necessary to save images to a removable disk in all situations. Thus, more data can remain on line for high-speed retrieval.

- **Redundant array of inexpensive disks (RAID):** Redundancy, or duplication, reduces the possibility of loss of data if a hard drive crashes, or loses its data. Because hard drives are used more often to store images, it is wise to employ a redundant system that has the same data on at least two hard drives. If data on one hard drive are destroyed or damaged, data that has been *mirrored,* or duplicated, on a second hard drive can be transferred to the first drive.

Disk technology offers high-speed searching and enormous storage capacity. The high-speed searching allows maximum efficiency by eliminating endless searching through file cabinets of paper documents, which can take hours. There is a massive reduction in storage space when optical disks are used. Disk technology has made and probably will continue to make a significant impact on the efficiency of image management.

Your Understanding

What is the difference between a real image and a data image?

Advantages of Disk Technology

- High-speed searching
- Large storage capacity

Data Images

Data images reduce paperwork and increase the speed of many operations required in a paper-based system. Data images are not exact likenesses of paper records but consist of selected information from paper records. Data images may be captured from paper by using scanners, or they may be captured directly from computer data.

Data Image Scanners

Types of data image scanners include bar code scanners, magnetic ink character recognition (MICR), optical character recognition (OCR), intelligent character recognition (ICR), and optical mask recognition (OMR).

Bar Coding Technology

A **bar code,** as illustrated in **Figure 11.6,** is a printed pattern of lines, or bars, which can be scanned and read. Each pattern of bars has a unique meaning. Bar coding technology is used to keep track of, sort, and distribute large volumes of paper records. For example, each bar code can represent a single document or file. A document printed with a bar code is read by a bar code scanner. The document can thus be tracked in a computer system according to when, where, and who borrowed the document from the files. It also enables the document to be sorted by a *bar code sorter,* or *BCS* (see **Figure 11.7**).

Figure 11.6

Bar code. *How many situations can you think of where bar codes are used?*

Figure 11.7

Bar code sorter.

Advantages of Bar Coding and Image Technology

- Decrease in overhead costs
- Decrease in consumer costs
- Increase in operational efficiency
- Increase in productivity

Bar code sorting has been used widely by the U.S. Postal Service. It has proven to be an efficient, cost-effective method of moving the mail. The following list compares the costs of bar coding (automation) to mechanical and manual methods of sorting for the U.S. Postal Service:

1. Manual: $35 per 1000 letters sorted.
2. Mechanization: $15 per 1000 letters sorted.
3. Bar coding (automation): $3 per 1000 letters sorted.

Bar coding technology decreases overhead costs while increasing operational efficiency. For example, if an organization uses a BCS, only one full-time employee is required to monitor the BCS. Fifty or more full-time employees would be needed to do the same job manually in the same amount of time. In addition, bar coding technology essentially eliminates data entry mistakes. Such errors contribute to costs because mistakes take extra time to correct. Increased productivity and decreased overhead costs are clear advantages to bar coding technology.

Image technology and bar coding systems can significantly increase operational efficiency and reduce overhead costs and consumer costs. Although the initial installation of one of these systems is expensive, it can pay for itself within one year. As technological developments continue, more and more paperwork will become "imagework."

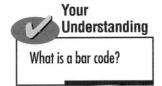

Your Understanding

What is a bar code?

Other Data Image Scanners

In addition to bar code scanners, other systems are used to read data from paper documents:

- **Magnetic ink character recognition:** Called **MICR,** this system is used largely by financial institutions to read magnetic characters on paper records such as checks.

- **Optical character recognition:** Referred to as OCR, this system can scan text pages and read printed characters to be input to computer memory. Reading accuracy is greater than 90 percent. Also used to capture real images.

- **Intelligent character recognition:** Abbreviated **ICR,** this system can scan handwriting and hand printing for computer input, but it is less accurate than OCR for reading.

- **Optical mask recognition:** Abbreviated **OMR,** this system scans only the parts of paper documents that are not blocked out, or masked. For example, a bank employee might want to read only the signature line of a check or signature card.

Computer Generated Output

Computer generated output means that reports are generated and sent directly to disk rather than being printed and later scanned. Reports on the disk can be viewed at a computer terminal. One system of computer-generated output is known as *computer output to laser disk,* or *COLD.*

Automated Records Management Systems

Businesses and organizations rely increasingly on information to compete and operate in a global economy. Such information takes many forms, as you have already learned. Information in the form of paper files, documents, and other records may be especially difficult to monitor and control because they are not accessible quickly by computer. Traditionally, such records have been tracked manually with log books, index card files, and printed lists of file captions.

More recently, computer programs known as **automated records management systems** have been developed to make files, documents, and other records accessible for management by computer. These systems can be used to track and analyze the status of individual documents. In this section, you will learn some of the major characteristics of automated records management systems. You will also determine how these systems are evaluated and selected.

Types of Automated Systems

Automated records management systems include *conventional systems* and *imaging* or *full-text systems.* Both types of systems require the use of software. Conventional systems usually do not require additional hardware. Nearly all businesses and organizations have their own computers. Using automated records management software, these computers can be used to track and analyze records at extraordinary

Types of Automated Systems

- Conventional
- Imaging or full-text

speeds. Information about records, but not their contents, can be viewed on the computer screen.

Imaging and full-text systems usually require additional hardware, such as optical character recognition (OCR) scanners. Unlike conventional systems, they permit the user to view and search on a computer screen the contents of records being tracked. Imaging and full-text systems are often used in the legal and medical fields because massive volumes of records must be monitored. Accuracy of records and speed of access are often critical.

The cost of an automated records management system can range from a few hundred to a half million dollars or more. ARMA's web site (www.arma.org/buyers/rm_software.httm) lists 62 records management software companies. The specific system to be purchased depends on the requirements for automated management, the type and size of the records management system already in place, and the budget available for automation. Once a need for automated records management has been established, three major considerations should be addressed: functions, cost, and architecture.

System Functions

The *functions* of a system are the operations the system will perform. Major functions available include:

- Management of all types of active records, including paper records, and computer disks.

- Management of inactive records in large records centers, including the tracking of inactive file containers or boxes.

- Management of archives, or valuable and historical records, that have a long retention period.

- Management of the full text of documents that are on electronic media.

- Management of records retention, which can include features such as automatic calculation of retention periods for all active and inactive records, identification of vital records, and notification and confirmation of records due for destruction.

Major Considerations for Automated Systems

- Functions
- Cost
- Architecture

System Functions for Management

- Active records
- Inactive records
- Archives
- Full-text documents
- Records retention
- Industry-specific records

- Management of records for a specific field such as law, medicine, and municipal government.

Required functions should be studied and decisions about them should be made before the factors of cost and architecture are considered. Remember that the purpose of converting to an automated system is increased operational efficiency and better service for those who access and use the records. In addition to the major functions listed above, the following features, available on many systems, should be investigated.

COMMAND-DRIVEN OR MENU-DRIVEN SYSTEM In a *command-driven system,* the user must enter keywords or instructions to operate the system. With a *menu-driven system,* items are selected with the click of a mouse from a list of choices or from pictures, called *icons,* on the screen.

TOGGLING With this feature the user can switch, or *toggle,* between one program and another without exiting either one.

BACKGROUND PROCESSES Systems having the *background processes* feature permit processes such as queries and indexing to be executed while the user performs other functions within the program.

BATCH PROCESSES The *batch processes* feature enables the user to process a group, or batch, of records at the same time.

GRAPHICAL USER INTERFACE A graphical user interface **(GUI)** (see **Figure 11.8**) enables the user to select screen options and operate the system by selecting graphic images, windows, forms, and icons with a mouse.

USER-DESIGNED CUSTOMIZATION The *user-designed customization* feature enables the user to specify the records structure, search parameters, report format, data entry screens, help messages, and language options (other than English).

FIELD DEFINITION With the *field definition* feature, the user can define fields to be string (alphanumeric, numeric, date, logical, or memo (text).

Feature Options

- Command or menu-driven system
- Toggling
- Background processes
- Batch processes
- Graphical user interface
- User-designed customization
- Field definition
- Global modifications
- Retrieval features
- Container management
- Request handling and reporting

Figure 11-8

Screen showing GUI images. *How are these images used on a typical computer?*

GLOBAL MODIFICATIONS A popular editing feature is the ability to make *global modifications,* which are additions or deletions made throughout the system with a single command.

RETRIEVAL FEATURES Some systems permit information to be searched and retrieved using a **keyword search,** which is any single word in a field. Others also allow retrieval by **phrase search,** defined as any two or more consecutive words in a field. A third type of retrieval is by **Boolean logic.** Boolean

Your Understanding

What is the purpose of automated records management systems?

logic searches are those using more than one keyword or phrase and a logic statement *(and, or, not, except, if, then)* to limit or expand the scope of the search. For example, the search command *Denver or Detroit* would retrieve all records pertaining to either of those two cities. The command *Denver and Detroit* would retrieve only the records pertaining to both Denver and Detroit.

To retrieve a record where only part of its identification is known requires the use of a **wildcard.** A wildcard is a symbol, such as an asterisk (*) or a question mark (?), used to represent any unknown character. An * represents an *unknown number* of characters, whereas each ? represents *one* unknown character. For example, the search command Schm* will cause retrieval of all surnames in the system beginning with the letters *Schm*, such as *Schmidt*, *Schmid*, and *Schmolitz*. The * is used because the number of letters that may follow *Schm* is unknown. To limit the search to names containing only two letters following *Schm*, the search command *Schm??* would be used. The positioning of the * or ? is also significant because it confines the search to characters in a certain position. If you were unsure of the prefix for the name MacLuddin or McLuddin, you would initiate your search with *Luddin. If you were trying to retrieve a telephone number whose three-digit area code is unknown, you would position the wild card in front of the phone number, *(???) 555-4209.*

CONTAINER MANAGEMENT Software with the *container management* feature can reserve space, determine available space, and monitor the contents of inactive file boxes and other containers.

REQUEST HANDLING AND REPORTING This feature can include several subfeatures. The principal function, *charge-out and return,* documents the loan of an item and notes its return. The *reservation* feature enables an item to be held for delivery on a specified date. The *waiting list* feature places a potential user on a list for records that have been charged out. The *charge-back* feature assigns the costs of loaning records back to a department or other unit.

System Costs

- Initial purchase and installation
- Maintenance and support of system
- Training of personnel

System Costs

After considering the functions of a system to be purchased, the RIM professional must give careful attention to the costs of the system. Total costs include the initial outlay plus long-term maintenance and support of the system, as well as training costs for employees who operate the system. Initial costs include payments for hardware, software, and installation. Long-term maintenance and support costs consist of data conversion fees, vendor support fees, system maintenance costs, and fees for software upgrades. Training costs include both vendor and user instructional programs. Other important cost considerations are product warranties, toll-free vendor telephone support, and free upgrades of software.

System Architecture

The *architecture* of a system refers to the characteristics of its hardware and software.

Factors include:

- The types of computers on which the software will run.

- The required computer operating system.

- The type of graphical user interface (GUI).

- The required type of network software.

- The programming language in which the software is written.

- Computer speeds and capacities; database capacities.

- Interfaces, or other applications that can be connected to the system, such as scanners, optical disk systems, and fax machines.

A careful study of system architecture features and requirements permits the RIM professional to determine whether or not the system will work with existing computer equipment. Such a study may reveal a need to purchase or lease new hardware and perhaps employ experts who can work with complex systems.

TERMS TO KNOW

▼

1. Review these key terms and important terms.
   - **architecture**
   - **automated records management system**
   - **background processes**
   - **bar code**
   - **bar code sorter (BCS)**
   - **batch processes**
   - **Boolean logic search**
   - **CD-R (compact disk-recordable)**
   - **CD-RW (compact disk-rewritable)**
   - **charge-back**
   - **charge-out and return**
   - **command-driven**
   - **computer-generated output**
   - **COLD (computer output to laser disk)**
   - **container management**
   - **conventional system**
   - **data image**
   - **disk technology**
   - **DVD (digital video [or versitale] disk)**
   - **field definition**
   - **functions**
   - **global modification**
   - **GUI (graphical user interface)**
   - **high speed image camera**
   - **icon**
   - **ICR (intelligent character recognition)**
   - **image technology**
   - **image scanner**
   - **imaging or full-text system**
   - **keyword search**
   - **menu-driven**
   - **MICR (magnetic ink character recognition)**

- microfiche
- microfilm
- microfilmer
- microform or microrecord
- mirrored
- OCR (optical character recognition)
- OMR (optimal mask recognition)
- phrase search
- RAID (redundant array of inexpensive disks)
- reader or viewer
- real image
- reader/printer
- reservation
- toggle
- user-designed customization
- waiting list
- wildcard search

2. Use each key term in a sentence. Underline or italicize each term.

DISCUSSION QUESTIONS

Answer each question as a written assignment or for class discussion. Be concise in your responses.

1. Define image technology.
2. What are the four major elements in any image technology system?
3. What is the difference between real and data images?
4. What is the difference between microfilm and microfiche?
5. How does an image scanner differ from a microfilmer?
6. What is the purpose of a microfilm reader?
7. What advantages does disk technology have over micrographic technology?

8. Name five kinds of disks used in disk technology.

9. What are the abbreviations for five types of data image scanners?

10. What kind of technology is used to keep track of, sort, and distribute large volumes of paper records?

11. What are two items of equipment used with bar coding technology?

12. Define computer-generated output.

13. Why might information in the form of files, documents, and other records be especially difficult to monitor?

14. What are the two types of automated records management systems, and how do they differ?

15. In what two professions are imaging and full-text systems often used?

16. What are three major considerations in choosing an automated records management system?

17. What features can automated management of records retention include?

18. What is the purpose of converting to an automated records management system?

19. If you want to change the name of a company wherever it appears in an automated system, what feature enables you to do so with a single command?

20. What do the total costs of an automated records management system include?

21. What are two reasons for carefully studying system architecture before purchasing an automated records management system?

CRITICAL THINKING

1. **Gather Facts**   Visit a store that uses a bar code scanner at the checkout.

   - Ask a manager or supervisor how the store tells its computer how much to charge for each bar coded item.

   - Ask how prices are changed in the system.

   Write a report on your findings.

2. **Generalize from Facts**   As a result of your store visit, write a statement about the advantages to both the store and the customer of the use of bar code technology.

3. **Create New Ideas**   Think of a possible new application of bar code technology that, as far as you know, has not yet been developed. Write a report about your suggestion.

NETWORKING WITH THE REAL WORLD

Consult with the librarian of your school as to whether or not books are ordered using e-commerce.

   - Access *Amazon.com*

   - Determine how books are ordered from that site.

   - As a group, decide whether or not you wish to place an order for a book related to your studies and, if so, order the book.

If you are using the workbook *Filing and Computer Database Projects,* you should have completed Database Project Five: Burger Barn, Assignments 33 through 40.

Safety, Security, and Disaster Recovery

The purpose of Chapter 12 is to enable you to:

- Enumerate ways of avoiding injuries in records areas.
- Identify several kinds of security devices for the protection of records and data.
- Describe disaster prevention measures for records storage areas.
- Identify methods of restoring records after a disaster.

KEY TERMS

- **authentication**
- **biometric access control device**
- **computer virus**
- **disaster recovery**
- **firewall**
- **human disaster**
- **natural disaster**
- **password**
- **scanner**
- **surge protector**
- **uninterruptible power source**
- **voice-input computer**

Although records storage areas are usually safe places to work, you can suffer injuries unless you follow important safety measures. One of the topics covered in this chapter is how to avoid such injuries. It is also essential to ensure the safety and security of the records themselves, an issue that is addressed in this chapter. Finally, if records are damaged because of a disaster, it is important to recover as much information as possible, which is the third major topic considered.

Avoiding Injuries in Records Areas

Sources of injury in records areas include (1) tripping, falling, or bumping into misplaced items or open file drawers; (2) electrical shock and tripping due to incorrect use of electrical devices and cords; (3) back injuries caused by lifting excessive weight or using incorrect lifting techniques; (4) head and body injuries caused by items falling from high shelves and storage cabinets; and (5) *repetitive motion injury,* which is damage to nerves and muscles caused by constant movement. An example of a repetitive motion injury sometimes suffered by records workers is *carpal tunnel syndrome. Carpal tunnel syndrome* is an injury of the wrist that can be caused by the repetitive motions of working at a computer keyboard.

The first step in avoiding injuries is to develop a written, comprehensive safety plan. The plan should include rules and regulations regarding the use of equipment as well as precautions to be followed when working in records storage areas. The next step is to train employees in how to follow the safety plan. Only after training should employees be allowed to work in records storage areas without supervision. Examples of specific policies you should comply with are listed below:

- Keep file drawers closed when they are not in use.
- Clear aisles and walkways of boxes and other materials such as electrical cords.
- Do not overload the top drawers of file cabinets. If a loaded top drawer is opened fully and the bottom drawers are empty, the cabinet could tip over—usually toward the file worker.
- Permit only trained electricians to install electrical equipment, including extension cords.
- Do not overload electrical circuits.
- Plug in and unplug electrical equipment only when the power switch is in the *off* position.
- To prevent back injuries, do not overload file boxes or containers. Lift items only within your limitations. Wear a back brace. Lift heavy objects on the floor from a squatting

Avoiding Injuries

- Develop written, comprehensive safety plan
- Train employees in this plan

Your Understanding

What should a RIM safety plan include?

position with the back straight. Do not bend from the waist to pick up a heavy object.

- Fasten file shelves and cabinets to the floor or wall if there is a possibility of top-heavy loading.

- Store heavy items on lower shelves of storage cabinets. Lighter items, which may be stored on top shelves, should be arranged carefully to prevent them from falling.

- Consider the use of an *ergonomic keyboard,* as shown in **Figure 12.1,** to reduce repetitive motion injuries caused by constant keyboard operation. Other options are to allow more time between keying activities and to use other input devices such as **scanners** and **voice-input computers** (see **Figures 12.2** and **12.3**).

Figure 12.1

Ergonomic keyboard.
What types of injury do you think the ergonomic keyboard was designed to reduce?

Figure 12.2

Scanner. *What types of things might you scan and for what purposes?*

Figure 12.3

Voice-input computer. *What types of situations can you think of where a voice-input computer might be used?*

Records Security

Security measures protect records from improper access, accidental loss, theft, damage, and unwanted destruction. The security of records and data can be jeopardized in many ways. Records can be misplaced, or they can be stolen by a competitor looking for trade secrets. They can be misused when they fall into the hands of employees or others who are not authorized to see them, or they can be burned, charred, scattered, and soaked as a result of natural or human disasters. Losing most or all of the records of an organization usually results in a large monetary loss not covered by insurance. In some cases, loss of important records results in a company going out of business.

Records Security

- Improper access
- Accidental loss
- Theft
- Damage
- Unwanted destruction

Security Systems

Organizations can improve the security of their paper and electronic records by installing one or more security systems for facility and data control. *Integrated security systems,* or *ISSs,* are methods of controlling access to facilities such as office buildings, floors, and rooms (see **Figure 12.4**). Integrated security systems include infrared invisible light beams, microwave sensors, and ultrasonic detectors. These systems can recognize body heat as well as movement in a targeted area and transmit the signal to a control panel.

Mechanical access control devices are traditional key-and-combination locks. They are often installed on important file cabinets and file shelves as well as office safes and records storage rooms.

Electronic access control devices use a computer system to control and monitor access to storage areas. *Smart cards* are compact disks (CDs) about the size of a credit card with a small

Figure 12.4

Integrated security system.

Figure 12.5

Electronic security card. *What should a card holder do if he or she were to lose the security card?*

microprocessor that can change the user's access number within a set time period. *Electronic security cards* look like a credit card with a magnetic strip on one side, as illustrated in **Figure 12.5.** *Electronic keys* are specially designed plastic passkeys without the grooves of traditional keys. Only employees who have been approved and cleared may use the card or key to unlock a storage area. They unlock the storage area by inserting the card or key into a slot next to the entrance. Each time the card or key is inserted, the employee's name and the time and date of access are recorded in a computer system.

Types of Security Systems

- Integrated security systems
- Mechanical access control devices
- Electronic access control devices
- Biometric access control devices
- Smoke and heat detectors
- Fire-resistant storage devices
- Sprinkler systems

Biometric access control devices, as illustrated in **Figure 12.6,** can evaluate unique physical characteristics of employees. If the characteristics evaluated match information in the system's memory, the employee is allowed access to a storage area or to computer data. Several types of biometric access control devices are *facial recognition,* the *fingerprint scanner,* the *handprint scanner,* the *retinal* or *iris eye pattern recognizer,* a *signature recognizer,* and the *voice-activated access system.* **Table 12.1** lists and describes each of these biometric access control devices.

Detectors can sense smoke and heat from fire. They can also perceive changes in levels of light, heat, and air conditioning and transmit electronic signals to security staff that notify them of adverse changes in the office environment. *Fire*

Figure 12.6

Biometric access control device (handprint scanner). *What are some advantages of using this device over an electronic security card scanning system?*

Table 12.1 Biometric Access Control Devices	
Biometric Access Control Device	**Description**
Facial recognition	Characteristics, such as the distance between facial features and the dimensions of the features, are measured and recorded. This information is stored as photographic images that are digitized, giving a numerical facial signature that is then matched when the person seeking admittance into the records storage area stands in front of a video camera.
Fingerprint scanner	A laser scans an employee's fingerprint when the finger is placed on an electro-optical plate. The computer system attached to the plate searches for a fingerprint match and allows access only for the person with a match.
Handprint scanner	Information about the three-dimensional size and shape of a hand is stored. When a person seeks access to the records storage area, he or she places a hand on a device that matches it against the stored image.
Retinal or iris eye pattern recognizer	A laser scans an employee's eye and attempts to find an eye pattern match within the computer system to determine if access to the storage area is allowed.
Signature recognizer	A person writes her or his signature on a digitized graphics tablet. Dynamics like speed, stroke order, and pressure are analyzed. The system compares the signature with stored information to determine if access is granted or denied.
Voice-activated access system	Prerecorded voice statements are loaded into a computer system. The system detects and matches voice patterns to identify employees who are allowed storage area access.

resistant storage devices include file cabinets and file shelves with insulation that protects the contents from various degrees of heat. *Sprinkler systems* are heat-sensitive devices installed in the ceiling of a building. They turn on automatically and spray water when they sense excess heat.

Before a records security system is selected, its potential benefits should be weighed carefully against its cost. Once purchased, the system must be properly installed and maintained, and employees must receive written procedures for using the system.

Electronic File Security

Electronic files can be lost or made available to unauthorized persons in several ways. In fact, electronic files may be at greater risk than paper files and equipment. Some of the risks to electronic files are listed:

- Failure to save a word processing or other type of file.

- Accidental erasure of a disk or other electronic medium.

- Misplaced or stolen floppy disks.

- Crashing of a computer hard disk.

- Damage to hardware and software from natural and human disasters.

- Electronic surveillance, or spying by competitors or others trying to gain information unfairly or trying to damage databases and other electronic information.

- Computer viruses.

Security for Electronic Files

- Surge protectors
- Battery-backup systems
- Authentication systems
- TEMPEST
- Black box technology
- Virus protection software

The following precautions will improve the security of electronic files significantly. *Surge protection* is a guard against file destruction caused by sudden changes in electrical current. A **surge protector,** illustrated in **Figure 12.7,** is a unit between the computer power cord and the electrical outlet. This unit can reduce electrical current overloads and thus prevent the destruction of data.

Figure 12.7

Surge protector. *What do you think might cause sudden changes in electrical current?*

Uninterruptible power sources, also called **UPS** or *battery backup systems,* provide standby power to a computer system in case of temporary electrical power loss.

Authentication systems protect the data in a computer or computer network by controlling user access. Only employees who correctly enter an identification code, or **password,** may view system data. Other higher level codes must be entered for employees to view *and* make changes in the data. These password codes are not to be shared with others, even if they have access to the system.

TEMPEST is the name for a federal government electronic signal emission standard. It may be adopted as a standard for all computer hardware. Such hardware resists electronic surveillance because special shields and coatings are used to deny unauthorized electronic access.

Black box technology involves the use of a communication security device that contains information about authorized users. Anyone using a correct access code and trying to gain access to a network is telephoned first. The telephone call verifies that the access request is authentic.

Virus protection software is a safeguard against **computer viruses,** or unwanted program instructions that can alter and destroy data. The virus protection program scans all the software in the system each time the computer is booted up. When a virus is found, the virus protection software provides on-screen instructions for removing the virus from the system.

Computer Network Security

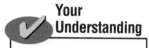

Your Understanding

How can electronic files be lost?

Companies using a network or the Internet should protect themselves against unauthorized access to their data. Most companies protect themselves by constructing a **firewall,** which enforces access control between networks by either blocking or permitting data transfer. Firewalls also enable companies to trace those trying to enter their computer system.

Sometimes sensitive data pass between a company and an outside source. For example, when you make a purchase on the Internet that requires a credit card, your account number passes from you to the vendor. You want your account number to be protected from access by outsiders. Two techniques are used to deal with this type of security issue: cryptography and authentication.

Cryptography allows users to send scrambled data to one another so others cannot read it. Cryptography also allows receivers of scrambled data to unscramble the data. Both parties use the same encryption software to scramble the data, and both parties have a key to unscramble it. The Internet vendor from whom you make a purchase uses data encryption to ensure that your credit card account number is protected. Companies that store their files on a server will use file encryption to ensure that no one outside can access those files. **Authentication** establishes who the users or other computers are and lets the computer system determine whether to allow access.

Disaster Preparedness

Businesses and organizations now pay greater attention than ever to the possibility of a catastrophic loss of records. This increased attention is spurred by the increased volume of records, the use of electronic databases that can be wiped out quickly, and the increased importance of records to the survival of the organization. Devastating losses, or disasters (**Figure 12.8**), are of two types: those caused by nature, called **natural disasters,** and those caused by people, called **human disasters.**

- Natural disasters: earthquakes, floods, hurricanes, tornadoes, some fires.
- Human disasters: arson, nuclear accidents, terrorism, civil disorder, hazardous materials accidents, equipment failure from neglect, vandalism, etc.

Figure 12.8

Disaster recovery in progress. *What steps should be in place to aid retrieving records after a disaster?*

Natural disasters cannot be prevented, but loss can be minimized. Disaster preparedness means being ready for natural disasters and having backup records in a location not likely to be affected by the disaster. Disaster preparedness also means trying to prevent human disasters and minimizing loss if they do occur.

As part of disaster preparedness, the records and information manager must first determine which documents are crucial for the survival of the organization. Once these documents are identified, three decisions are made:

Considerations for Vital Documents

- What should their format be?
- Where should they be kept?
- How secure should the off-site location be?

1. **What should be the format of the vital documents?** Microforms and document imaging are common methods of protection for important records. Copies of the originals can be stored at the office, while the microforms (or image diskettes) and the originals can be stored at a highly controlled off-site location. Computer records should be backed up onto disk or tape. Many organizations use the grandfather/father/son *backup* method: the most recent data (son) are kept either on site or at a remote location; yesterday's data (father) are rotated to a different location; and the prior day's data (grandfather) are rotated to yet another remote location. The prudent organization holds regular practice drills to ensure that it can always recover vital data.

2. **Where should the records be located?** It may be desirable to locate backup records off site. Some records professionals choose an off-site location many miles from the base office site. This precaution is taken so that if a natural disaster hits, it is unlikely that the remote site would also be hit.

3. **How secure should the off-site location be?** Some off-site locations for records storage have specially designed rooms or vaults with temperature and humidity control. Some are in underground caves or tunnels. Fire protection at some sites includes a sprinkler system that sprays an inert gas, halon, instead of water.

Halon causes minimal damage to records compared with water.

Some sites provide the special service of *electronic vaulting:* storing backup copies of vital electronic records.

Disaster Recovery

Once a disaster happens, the RIM professional executes plans for saving as many records as possible, an activity called **disaster recovery.** It is not likely that many records will be saved if they have been exposed to the heat, smoke, and flames of a serious fire. Backup records stored at an off-site location will have to replace those destroyed in a fire.

Paper records can be recovered from water damage in unique ways. For document restoration, it is important to remove all standing water as soon as possible.

Two techniques used to dry out water-soaked records are freeze-drying and air-drying. The *freeze-drying technique* requires placing the records in a freezer and blasting in surges of cold air, (usually at −20°F). Once the documents are frozen, they are placed in a freeze-drying chamber, where vacuum pressure causes the frozen water in the paper to evaporate without returning to its liquid state.

With the *air-drying technique,* documents are separated and placed individually on polyester webbing. The webbing and documents are then hung in a well-ventilated room so the water will evaporate.

Wet-paper recovery works only if put into action immediately after the disaster. Mold will begin to accumulate on paper that is left standing longer than forty-eight hours.

Magnetic media can also be recovered from water damage. Most electronic records can be restored successfully if correct actions are taken within seventy-two to ninety-six hours of damage. Open-reel tapes and cartridges exposed to heavy water damage must be dried individually with special electronic equipment. Using the same equipment, floppy disks can be dried in bulk at high speed.

> **Disaster Recovery of Records**
>
> - Fire — heat, smoke and flames; little chance of recovery
> - Water — good chance of recovery by freeze-drying and/or air-drying

Your Understanding

What are considered human disasters?

TERMS TO KNOW

▼

1. Review these key terms and important terms.

- air-drying technique
- authentication system
- battery-backup system
- biometric access control device
- black box technology
- carpel tunnel syndrome
- computer virus
- cryptography
- detector
- disaster recovery
- electronic access control device
- electronic key
- electronic security card
- electronic vaulting
- ergonomic keyboard
- facial recognition
- fingerprint scanner
- firewall
- fire-resistant storage device
- freeze-drying technique
- handprint scanner
- human disaster
- integrated security system (ISS)
- mechanical access control device
- natural disaster
- password
- repetitive motion injury
- retinal or iris eye-pattern recognizer
- signature recognizer
- scanner
- smart cards
- sprinkler system
- surge protector
- TEMPEST
- uninterruptible power source (UPS)
- virus protection software
- voice-activated access system
- voice-input computer

2. Assume that each key term is the answer to a question. Write a question for each answer.

DISCUSSION QUESTIONS

▼

Answer each question as a written assignment or for class discussion. Be concise in your responses.

1. What is the first step in avoiding injuries in the records workplace?

2. What might happen to a file cabinet if a loaded top drawer is opened fully and its bottom drawers are empty?

3. What should you check before you plug in an item of electrical equipment?

4. What are three ways to reduce repetitive motion injuries caused by constant keyboard operation?

5. Records security measures protect records from what types of risks?

6. What can biometric access control devices evaluate before permitting access to facilities or data?

7. What should the RIM professional do before selecting a records security system?

8. Name at least three of the risks to electronic files.

9. What is the purpose of an authentication system?

10. What kind of damage can a computer virus inflict on computer data?

11. Why do organizations now give more attention than ever to the possibility of a catastrophic loss of records?

12. What does disaster preparedness mean?

13. What do we call the activity of saving as many records as possible after a disaster?

14. What are two techniques for recovering paper records from water damage?

CRITICAL THINKING

1. **Gather Facts** Use various resources, including the Internet, to research the present and projected use of voice-input technology. Prepare a brief report on your findings.

2. **Generalize from Facts** Determine and list the advantages of voice-input data entry over manual keyboard entry of data.

3. **Create New Ideas** Envision one or more novel uses of voice-input technology that would be helpful to you in your everyday activities. Report orally on your recommendations in a group discussion.

NETWORKING WITH THE REAL WORLD

Access *Monster.com.* The address is http://www.monster.com. Using this resource, find a job that interests you. Write a letter of application for the job.

IMPLEMENTING UNIT 3 CONCEPTS

GROUP ACTIVITY

Design and develop a database for the students in your educational institution. Publish an alphabetized directory of all students.

The database might include information about the student such as:

1. Name

2. Address

3. Student identification number

4. Phone number

5. Class schedule

Before you begin to design your database, record additional information you would like to see included in the database.

INDIVIDUAL INQUIRY

Interview someone who works with electronic files. From this Interview, you should determine:

- How data are protected from loss.

- How data re protected from unauthorized access.

Report your findings to the class.

Sample questions you might ask of the interviewee are:

1. Are passwords used?

2. How are data backed up?

3. Are there different levels of access?

4. Have data been lost in the past?

5. Have you had any other problems with the electronic files in your organization?

Before you begin your interview, identify several questions you could include in your interview.

SYNTHESIZING UNIT 3 CONCEPTS

GROUP ACTIVITY

Obtain information from local government officials such as firefighters, emergency workers, and police officers about their experiences in assisting with disaster recovery of paper and electronic records. Determine from these government officials the following information and report your findings to the class:

1. What are the mistakes people and organizations make that cause them to lose business records?

2. What recommendations can they make to avoid such loss.?

INDIVIDUAL INQUIRY

Select an organization or business that uses one or more electronic databases. Follow these procedures to perform and document a study of that company's database system.

1. Meet with a person in the organization who is familiar with the system and obtain information about the system.

2. Study the system in detail.

3. List any recommendations that resulted from your study.

4. Discuss the recommendations with the management of the organization.

5. After your interview, prepare a report of your findings and include the management's reaction to your recommendations.

Note: Questions you can ask for Item 2 might include but not be limited to the following:

1. How was the system designed?

2. What data are included?

3. How is the system used?

4. What security measures are followed?

5. Are disaster preparedness plans in place?

6. Are there any problems with the system?

Additional Indexing and Alphabetizing Practice

Following are twelve lists to be indexed and alphabetized, one for each filing rule (see pages 46–62, Chapter 5). (1) Write or key each name in indexed order. (2) Show the alphabetical order of the names by writing 1 at the left of the first name, 2 at the left of the second, and so on. Present your work in the same format as illustrated in Chapter 5.

Rule 1

5 Farrah Kahn
3 Agnes Bankson
2 Andy R. Banks
4 Aaron Bankston
1 R. April Bankhead

Rule 2

5 Leah FitzGerald
1 Suzette Dearmon
3 Lee Ann FitzCharles
2 Annette DeArmond
4 LeRoy FitzCharles

Rule 3

5 Maria Perez-Perales
1 Vanessa Elam
3 Ricardo Perez
2 Mohamed El-Amin
4 Rosa M. Perez-Garza

Rule 4

5 Eliz. Redmond
2 Robt. Quintero
4 Betty Redmond
3 Ben Red-Bear
1 Robert A. Quintero

Rule 5

3 Brook Washington, Jr.
2 Amelia Rossi, M.D.
5 Mrs. Brook Washington
1 Mayor Amelia Rossi
4 Lt. Brook Washington

Rule 6

Adams Pallet Company
Waller County Daily News
Western Dude Ranch
A Touch of Class Boutique
The Wall Street Journal

Rule 7

J. Edward Henry and Assoc.
Westside Mfg. Co.
Henry and Chan, Ltd.
Westheimer Corp.
Thomas Sign Co.

Rule 8

Diana's Boutique

X-Ray Inspection, Inc.

XL Engineering Co.

D'Amico's Pasta House

X-Pressions

Rule 9

24 Hour Wrecker Service

Three T Motors

3 Star Theater

Twenty-nine Palms Restaurant

300 South Ivy Apartments

Rule 10

The Low % Loan Agency

Dollar Rent A Car

A #1 Washeteria

C & F Fashions

$ Daze Savings Place

Rule 11 (State and Local Government Names)

Board of Tax Appeals

City of Buena Vista, VA

Bureau of Finance

State of Ohio

Columbus, OH

Rule 11 (United States Government Names)

U.S. Treasury Department
Internal Revenue Service

U.S. Department of Interior
National Park Service

Rule 11 (Foreign Government Names)

Department of Fisheries
Uruguay

Ministry of the Arts
Turkey

Rule 12

Sam's Seafood
695 Front Street
Crowley, VT

Sam's Seafood
2 Front Street
Crowley, VT

Sam's Seafood
19 Fox La.
Detroit, MI

Professional Associations

American Management Association
135 West 50th Street
New York, NY 10020
www.amanet.org

Association for Systems Management
2487 Bagley Road
Cleveland, OH 44138
www.auburn.edu/student_info/asm/asmindex.html

Association of Information and Image Management
1100 Wayne Avenue, Suite 1100
Silver Spring, MD 20910
www.aiim.org

Association of Records Managers and Administrators Inc.
4200 Somerset, Suite 215
Prairie Village, KS 66208
www.arma.org

Data Management Association
505 Busse Highway
Park Ridge, IL 60068
www.dama.org

Institute of Certified Records Managers
P.O. Box 8188
Prairie Village, KS 66208
www.mindspring.com

International Records Management Trust
12 John Street
London WCIN 2EB, UK
www.irmt.org

National Archives And Records Administration (NARA)
700 Pennsylvania Ave, Nw
Washington, DC 20408
www.nara.gov

National Association of Government Archives and Records
 Administrators (NAGARA)
48 Howard St.
Albany, NY 12207
Nagara@caphill.com

Professional Records and Information Services Management
 International (PRISM International)
16 E. Rowan St., Suite 400
Raleigh, NC 27609
www.prismintl.org

Society of American Archivists
500 Wells St, 5th Floor
Chicago, IL 60607
www.archivists.org

Professional Publications

American Archivist
> The Society of American Archivists
> 600 S Federal, Suite 504
> Chicago, IL 60605
> www.archivists.org

Beyond Computing
> International Business Machines Corporation
> Old Orchard Road
> Armonk, NY 10504
> www.beyondcomputingmag.com

Clearinghouse News and Reports on Government Records
> NAGARA
> 48 Howard St.
> Albany, NY 12207
> Nagara@caphill.com (email address)

Document World Magazine
> AIIM (Association of Information and Image Management)
> 1100 Wayne Avenue, Suite 1100
> Silver Spring, MD 20910
> www.aim.org

InFocus
> PRISM'S Quarterly Journal
> 16 E. Rowan St., Suite 400
> Raleigh, NC 27609
> www.prismintl.org

InfoPro
   ARMA International (available only to members)
   4200 Somerset Dr., Suite 215
   Prairie Village, KS 66208-5287
   www.arma.org

Inform
   AIIM
   11600 College Blvd., Suite 100
   Overland Park, KS 66210
   www.aiim.org

The Information Management Journal
   ARMA International
   4200 Somerset, Suite 215
   Prairie Village, KS 66208
   www.arma.org

Keys to Chapter 5 and Appendix A

CHAPTER 5 KEY

Rule 1 Workout

_3_ Moore Jerry D
_5_ Valentino L Teresa
_2_ Lamb Charles
_4_ Valentine Ross Will
_1_ Lam Tony

Rule 2 Workout

_1_ OBrien Lisa S
_5_ VonderBusch Frederick
_3_ ONeal Richard
_4_ Vonderahe Gus
_2_ Oneal Martin

Rule 3 Workout

_1_ HarperHuff Lloyd Ray
_5_ Wong Lynette
_4_ Wong LuLynn
_3_ Wong Luke
_2_ Jones Patrick

Rule 4 Workout

_1_ Alvarez Wm G

_3_ DAgostino Christine

_4_ Kahn Lou

_5_ Kahn Louis

_2_ DAgostino Chas

Rule 5 Workout

_5_ Sahbie Ahmad R Dr

_1_ Lloyd James A Rev

_4_ LopezDeVilla Linda CPA

_3_ LopezDevilla Linda

_2_ Lloyd James R

Rule 6 Workout

_3_ Parsell Furniture Company

_5_ Simmons and Conner

_1_ Master Locksmiths

_4_ Paul Simmons Corporation

_2_ Mister Submarine Cafe

Rule 7 Workout

_5_ Micro Specialties Inc

_3_ Garden Supplies Co

_1_ Farris Service Center Inc

_4_ Garza and Gravley Attys

_2_ Fashion Corner Etc

Rule 8 Workout

_5_ Saras HotDogs Inc

_3_ Sam the Barber

_1_ Lil Rascals Day Care

_4_ Sams Fried Chicken

_2_ Lillys Florist

Rule 9 Workout

_3_ 4 Mockingbirds Café

_4_ First Impressions Hairstyles

_2_ 4 Columns Inn

_1_ 1 Choice Auto Auction

_5_ One Lakeland Villa

Rule 10 Workout

_5_ Rogers and Kirk Co The

_4_ Nunez and Kelly

_1_ High Dollar Real Estate Agcy

_3_ Number 1 Motor Sales

_2_ M and M Food Store

Rule 11 Workout (State and Local Government Names)

_3_ Sheridan City of
    Social Services Department of
    Sheridan Wyoming

_1_ Perry City
    Personnel Department
    Perry Missouri

_2_ Perry County
    Medical Examiner
    Hazard Kentucky

Rule 11 Workout (United States Government Names)

_2_ United States Government
    Interior Department
    National Park Service

_1_ United States Government
    Commerce Department
    Census Bureau

_3_ United States Government
    Treasury Department
    Engraving and Printing Bureau of

Rule 11 Workout (Foreign Government Names)

_1_ Australia
    State Department of

_2_ Germany
    Consulate General

_3_ Peru
    Industrial Development Authority

Rule 12 Workout

_3_ Videoworld Toledo Ohio Oak Street 257

_1_ Videoworld Toledo Ohio Norris Avenue 110

_2_ Videoworld Toledo Ohio Norris Avenue 1400

_4_ Videoworld Union Montana Ardmore Drive 37

APPENDIX A KEY

Rule 1

_5_ Kahn Farrah

_3_ Bankson Agnes

_2_ Banks Andy R

_4_ Bankston Aaron

_1_ Bankhead R April

Rule 2

_5_ Fitzgerald Leah

_1_ Dearmon Suzette

_3_ FitzCharles Lee Ann

_2_ DeArmond Annette

_4_ FitzCharles LeRoy

Rule 3

_5_ PerezPearles Maria

_1_ Elam Vanessa

_3_ Perez Ricardo

_2_ ElAmin Mohamed

_4_ PerezGarza Rosa M

Rule 4

_5_ Redmond Eliz

_2_ Quintero Robt

_4_ Redmond Betty

_3_ RedBear Ben

_1_ Quintero Robert A

Rule 5

_3_ Washington Brook Jr

_2_ Rossi Amelia MD

_5_ Washington Brook Mrs

_1_ Rossi Amelia Mayor

_4_ Washington Brook Lt

Rule 6

_2_ Adams Pallet Company

_4_ Waller County Daily News

_5_ Western Dude Ranch

_1_ A Touch of Class Boutique

_3_ Wall Street Journal The

Rule 7

_2_ J Edward Henry and Assoc

_5_ Westside Mfg Co

_1_ Henry and Chan Ltd

_4_ Westheimer Corp

_3_ Thomas Sign Co

Rule 8

_2_ Dianas Boutique

_5_ XRay Inspection Inc

_3_ XL Engineering Co

_1_ DAmicos Pasta House

_4_ XPressions

Rule 9

_2_ 24 Hour Wrecker Service

_4_ Three T Motors

_1_ 3 Star Theater

_5_ Twentynine Palms Restaurant

_3_ 300 South Ivy Apartments

Rule 10

_5_ Low Percent Loan Agency The

_4_ Dollar Rent A Car

_1_ A Number1 Washeteria

_2_ C and F Fashions

_3_ Dollar Daze Savings Place

Rule 11 (State and Local Government Names)

_1_ Buena Vista City of
Tax Appeals Board of
Buena Vista Virginia

_2_ Ohio State of
Finance Bureau of
Columbus Ohio

Rule 11 (United States Government Names)

_2_ United States Government
Treasury Department
Internal Revenue Service

_1_ United States Government
Interior Department of
National Park Service

Rule 11 (Foreign Government Names)

_2_ Uruguay
Fisheries Department of

_1_ Turkey
Arts Ministry of the

Rule 12

_2_ Sams Seafood Crowley Vermont Front Street 695

_1_ Sams Seafood Crowley Vermont Front Street 2

_3_ Sams Seafood Detroit Michigan Fox La 19

access   The component of retrieval in which employees obtain information that is stored.

access rights   Settings placed on folders and files that control which users on the LAN have permission to view, modify, or delete a particular electronic record.

ADA   Americans with Disabilities Act; contains requirements about accessibility to equipment by persons who have disabilities.

address   An identifier assigned to a computer that is unique on the network; all messages to a particular computer must use its address.

admissibility into evidence   Refers to whether or not a photocopy, microfilm copy, or computer software copy of a document will be accepted in court as valid evidence in a lawsuit.

air-drying technique   Removing water from soaked documents by placing them on polyester webbing and allowing the water to evaporate.

alias   Another name for a shortcut or link.

alphabetic filing   Organizing records according to the sequence of letters in the alphabet.

alphabetizing   Arranging names in alphabetic order.

alphanumeric   A field type that can include alphabetic characters, numbers, and other keyboard characters; same as *string*.

AND   In programming and searching, AND means that all the conditions must be true for the result to be true.

application   A program. A set of instructions that the computer must follow to read and modify electronic records.

architecture   Characteristics of hardware and software used in an automated system.

archival management   The maintenance of archives.

archives   Groups of records, usually valuable and historical, that are not referred to in the day-to-day operations of the organization.

archivist   A job title for a person who maintains archives.

ARMA International   Association of Records Managers and Administrators.

associate   The operating system pairs a file type with the application used to create it so a user can open and manipulate the file without having to open the application first.

attachment   A document that accompanies an e-mail message

authentication   A system for protecting the data on a computer or computer network by controlling user access

automated records management system   Software program that makes files, documents, and other records accessible to management by computer.

background processes   A systems feature that permits processes such as queries and indexing to be executed while the user performs other functions within the program.

backup n. An electronic copy of data, usually captured on disk or tape and kept in a remote location for disaster recovery. *v.* The process of making a copy of part or all of a computer's electronic records for archival storage.

bar code Patterns of bars, or lines, that have a unique meaning and represent a single document or file.

bar code sorter (BCS) A machine that arranges documents by reading bar codes.

batch processes A system feature in which a group of records can be processed at once.

battery-backup system Provides standby power to a computer system in case of temporary electrical power loss.

biometric access control device A mechanism that can evaluate the unique physical characteristics of employees for security purposes.

black box technology The use of a communication security device that contains information about authorized users.

Boolean logic search Query using more than one keyword or phrase and a logic statement *(and, or, not, except, if, then)* to limit or expand the scope of the search.

browser An application that allows you to see all of the root folders and their folders and files.

business forms Business records that have blank spaces to be filled in.

by-product information A group of facts created for a secondary reason.

byte A single electronic character.

carpal tunnel syndrome An injury of the wrist that can be caused by the repetitive motions of working at a computer keyboard.

case Refers to whether letters of the alphabet are written in small (lowercase) letters (a) or in capital (uppercase) letters (A).

CD-RW Compact disk-rewritable; a compact disk onto which new data can be recorded over old data.

CD-W Compact disk-writable; a relatively inexpensive compact disk onto which data can be recorded once.

charge-back A system feature that assigns costs of loaning records to a department or other unit.

charge-out and return The principal function of the request-handling-and-reporting feature; documents the loan of an item and notes its return.

chronological file A storage location for records in which the records are arranged in order according to the date they are to be acted on.

chronological order Order by date.

civil laws Laws covering legal disputes between one individual or business and another.

client A computer that requests information from other computers; usually a desktop computer that one person uses to do her or his work or look up information.

command-driven System operation method in which the user must enter keywords or instructions.

computer An electronic device for creating, storing, manipulating, and performing calculations on data using a set of instructions.

computer generated output   Imaging method in which reports are generated and sent directly to disk rather than being printed and later scanned.

console emulation   Using one computer to behave as if it were the screen, keyboard, and mouse of another. This technique is usually accomplished with an application such as pcAnywhere and a modem or network connection.

container management   A system feature that can reserve space, determine available space, and monitor the contents of inactive file boxes and other containers.

contract   An agreement between two parties that sets forth the expectations for each side.

conventional system   Automated system that usually does not require the purchase of additional hardware.

copy   Computer output to laser disk system of computer-generated output.

copyright   An exclusive right granted by the government for the production, publication, or sale of an artistic, musical, or literary work.

country code   A two-letter TLD indicating a domain's geographic location.

CPU   Central processing unit; the part of the computer that does all of the actual calculating.

criminal laws   Laws covering legal disputes between the government and an individual or business.

criteria   Requirements specified to find a file when doing a search.

CRM   Certified records manager.

cross-reference   A notation that a name or record is filed elsewhere.

cryptography   Allows users to send scrambled data to one another so others cannot read it.

cut   The width of a folder or guide tab relative to the width of the folder or guide.

data image   Information, rather than a picture, that is captured from paper and converted to electronic form.

database   A body of organized data, usually managed in a computer system, that can be modified, reorganized, and accessed in various ways to carry out administrative tasks and solve business problems.

database management system   The database application that allows you to create (DBMS) and use a database.

date   A field type that contains a date or time.

DBMS   Abbreviation for database management system.

delivery   The component of retrieval in which requested records are conveyed to the user.

depository   A location similar to a records center but usually a part of the organization rather than a separate business. Can also be referred to as a repository.

detector   Device that can sense smoke and heat from fire. Some detectors can also perceive changes in levels of light, heat, and air conditioning.

dictionary subject files   Files that are in alphabetic order by main subject headings with no subheadings.

digital signature   The digital equivalent of a signature; it can be placed on a document by a special application program that creates a unique string of digits to be identified by the recipient who must have a program to interpret it.

directory   Also called a folder; a type of container that holds other folders and files.

disaster recovery   Executing plans for saving as many records as possible after a disaster.

disintegrator   A machine that chops materials into small pieces.

disk technology   The use of computer disks to store real images.

documentation   The component of retrieval that uses an out guide to account for the whereabouts of a record.

domain name   A name given to a computer residing on the Internet; all domain names have at least two parts: the organization or company, and the type of organization or country of origin.

DVD   Digital video disk; an emerging technology that may replace conventional compact disk technology.

electronic access control device   Mechanism that uses a computer system to control and monitor access to storage areas.

electronic file system   The combination of computer hardware, software, and operating system that allows information to be stored and organized in a logical and usable way on a computer.

electronic key   An electronic access control device; a specially designed plastic passkey that has no grooves like traditional keys.

electronic security card   Electronic control access device that looks like a credit card with a magnetic strip on one side.

electronic vaulting   Storing backup copies of vital electronic records in off-site locations or specially designed rooms or vaults where temperature and humidity are controlled.

ELF   "Eliminate Legal Files"; a campaign by ARMA to eliminate legal-size files and legal-size paper.

e-mail   Electronic mail; a means of sending a message or other document from one computer to one or more other computers.

encyclopedic subject files   Files that are in alphabetic order by main subject headings, many of which have subheadings.

ergonomic keyboard   Input device similar to a traditional keyboard but uniquely designed to lessen repetitive motion injuries.

ergonomics   The applied science of conforming equipment, systems, and the working environment to the require-ments of people, including those who have disabilities.

facial recognition   A biometric access control device that reads facial characteristics.

fax   A copy of a document sent from one facsimile machine to another over telephone lines.

field   One category of information storage that cannot be broken down further; examples are name, date hired, part number.

field definition   A feature that can be used to define fields as character, numeric, date, logical, or memo (text).

file   An electronic record stored on the computer that uses a filename for reference; a single file is associated with one or more applications that can read and modify it.

file folder   Heavy paper container for filed records.

file guide   Cardboard divider used to support folders and identify file sections.

file label   Small self-adhesive tag used to identify folders and guides; tag inserted in rectangular frame at the front of a file drawer and used to identify contents of the drawer.

file server   A computer that acts as a central repository for all important electronic records in a company or department. Individual desktop computers access the files through the network and save them on the file server.

file type   A two-to four-letter code added to the filename (after a .) so the computer knows which application can read the file. File types generally should not be changed by the user.

filename   The human readable caption given to an electronic record or document.

filing equipment   Consists primarily of file containers, cabinets, and filing accessories.

filing supplies   Folders for paper records and accessories such as file dividers and labels.

fingerprint scanner   A biometric access control device that reads fingerprints.

fire-resistant storage device   File cabinets and file shelves with insulation that protects the contents from various degrees of heat.

firewall   A device used to enforce access control between computer networks by blocking or permitting data flow.

folder   Also called a directory; a type of container that holds other folders and files.

follow-up   The component of retrieval in which records employees remind users that borrowed records are to be returned.

follow-up file   Another term for a chronological file.

form   An input and display window on the computer screen that allows record fields to be positioned and labeled in a way that makes entry and retrieval of information easier for the computer operator.

form-filling software   Computer programs that enable users to fill in business forms using a computer printer instead of a typewriter.

forms-design software   Computer software that helps users to design efficient business forms at the computer.

freeze-drying technique   Removing water from soaked records by first freezing them and then allowing the ice to evaporate.

full backup   A backup containing a complete copy of every file.

functions   Operations the system will perform.

general caption   A caption that signals the location of an accumulation of records with varying subject captions.

geographic filing   Organizing records by locality, area, or territory.

gigabyte   1024 megabytes (1,073,741,824 bytes)

global modification   Addition or deletion made throughout a system with a single command.

Graphical User Interface (GUI)   Enables the user to select screen options and operate the system with a keyboard, mouse, or other input device, that points to graphical images, windows, forms, and icons.

handprint scanner   A biometric access control device that reads the shape and size of a hand.

hard copy   Computer output printed on paper.

hard copy mail   Any kind of paper mail.

hard drive   Also hard disk; permanent storage device for the operating system, application programs, documents, and records used by a computer on a regular basis.

hardware   The physical parts of a computer system such as the CPU, keyboard, monitor, disk drives, mouse, and printer.

high-speed image camera   Another name for an image scanner.

html   Hypertext markup language. A document's file type.

http   Hypertext transfer protocol; a method for communicating on the Internet that allows retrieval of text, images, and sound documents.

human disaster   Catastrophe caused by people.

hyperlink   The ability to use part of a document as a link (or shortcut) to another document. Special codes entered in a Web page document give the Web browser the address of another Internet document. When the person clicks on the words or picture, the Web-browser displays the linked document; a pointer that allows you to jump to another location, such as another file on your hard disk, your company's network, or an Internet address.

icon   Screen picture selected by keys or a mouse to operate a system that is menu-driven.

ICR   Intelligent character recognition; a system that can scan handwriting and hand printing for computer input but with less reading accuracy than OCR.

ICRM   Institute of Certified Records Managers.

image scanner   A machine into which paper documents are fed for conversion to electronic form, usually onto one of several types of disks.

image technology   The conversion of paper records to photographic or electronic form and the administration of the new form.

imaging or *full-text system*   Automated system that usually requires the purchase of additional hardware such as optical character recognition (OCR) scanners. Unlike conventional systems, this system permits the user to view and search on a computer screen the contents of records being tracked.

incinerate   To destroy records by burning them.

incoming paperwork   Paperwork that arrives from sources outside the organization.

incremental backup   A backup containing only the changes made since the last incremental or full backup.

indexing   Determining the order and format of the units in a name when alphabetizing.

indirect system   A filing system that requires reference to an index before the records can be located. Numeric filing is an indirect system.

information system   How businesses and other organizations plan, develop, and organize their information.

input device   Computer hardware devices that allow people to enter information into a computer; keyboard, mouse, and microphone are examples.

integer   A number that can only be a whole number; 1, 5, −30 are integer numbers.

integrated security system (ISS)   Method of controlling access to facilities such as office buildings, floors, and rooms.

internal paperwork   Paperwork that is sent by fax or messenger from one office of the organization to another.

Internet   A network of networks that allows a computer to exchange information with computers all over the world.

intranet   An organizational version of the Internet where documents are available only to computers within the company.

key   A field within a table whose value is unique within a table. It is used to relate a record to one or more records in another table.

keyword search   Using any single word in a field to find a record.

kilobyte   1024 bytes

link   Same as a shortcut or alias; a type of field that refers (or links) to an external, usually large, file.

litigation   The act of engaging in a civil lawsuit.

local area network (LAN)   A network that connects computers in a company or organization.

logical   A type of field that can have only one of two values, for example, Yes or No.

lowercase   Characters of the alphabet written as small letters.

mapped drive   The creation of a semipermanent connection to another computer, usually a file server, by assigning it to a drive letter in a desktop operating system.

mechanical access control device   Traditional key or combination lock.

megabyte   1024 kilobytes

memo   A field type that can hold up to 64 K of text; used for adding comments to a record.

menu-driven   System operation method in which a keyboard or a mouse is manipulated to select items from a list of choices or icons on the screen.

metadata   Information about information; a description of facts about a particular electronic record such as the last access date, the author, and the last print time.

metasearch   Searching the Internet by using words or phrases to request a Web search from several search engines and returning the links to the documents they find.

method   A protocol used for communicating with a server and thus moving information across the Internet.

MICR   Magnetic ink character recognition; system used largely by financial institutions to read magnetic characters on paper records, such as checks, as a means of data imaging.

microfiche   A flat, transparent film sheet containing microforms.

microfilm   A 16-mm, 35-mm, or 105-mm roll of film containing microforms.

microfilmer   A camera specially designed to take pictures of documents onto microfilm or microfiche.

microform (microrecord)   A miniature picture of a single paper record on a microfilm roll or microfiche.

mirrored   Data that are duplicated on one or more disks. A redundant system to protect data in the event of a hard-drive crash.

natural disaster   Catastrophe caused by nature.

natural language search   A way of searching the Internet by asking questions.

network   A group of computers linked together electronically; a set of cables (or media), protocols, and equipment that allows computers to communicate directly with one another.

network database   A database that is accessed by many people through the company's network or the World Wide Web.

network equipment   The specialized computers and components that translate signals into useful information so that electronic messages can be sent from one computer to another. It includes hubs and routers as well as the ethernet cards that exist in the computers using the network.

network media   Cables, fiber-optics, and radio waves used to move electronic information from one computer to another.

nonrecord   Document that is more expensive to keep than to discard.

normalization   In database design, making sure all fields within a table correspond to the key value of the table on a one-to-one basis.

number   A numeric value; a field that will be used in mathematical computations.

numeric filing   Organizing records according to preassigned or assigned numbers.

object   A type of field that can hold any amount of information of any type, including a program. The database assumes that the operating system will handle any manipulation of the object.

OCR   Optical character recognition; the technology of using image scanners to convert an image of text into computer-editable text.

OMR   Optical mask recognition; a system that scans only the parts of paper documents that are not blocked out, or masked.

operating system   A program that allows the application program to communicate with each piece of hardware. Applications cannot be run and records cannot be stored on a computer without an operating system.

OR   In programming and searching, an OR means that if any of the conditions are true, then the result is true.

out guide   A heavy paper signpost that documents the location from which a record was removed, the name of the record, the borrower, the date it was borrowed, and the date the record is due to be returned.

outgoing paperwork Copies kept of documents that were sent outside the organization.

output device Computer hardware that presents information to people. A printer and monitor are examples.

password The identification code used as part of an authentication system.

path The combination of folder names and filename that define the address of an Internet document.

peer A computer that both requests and gives information. Computers that run videoconferencing or "chat" software act as peers for the computers with which they are communicating.

phrase search Using two or more consecutive words in a field to find a record.

pointer A hyperlink that allows you to jump to another location, such as another file on your hard disk, your company's network, or an Internet address.

program A set of instructions for a computer.

protocol A set of rules that allows one computer to send and receive information from another.

pulping A process used to destroy records by adding water and creating a slurry mixture.

query A set of rules for selecting records that meet specific criteria from a database.

RAID Redundant array of inexpensive disks; redundancy, or duplication, reduces the possibility of loss of data if a hard drive crashes.

RAS Abreviation for *remote access service*. This Microsoft Windows application allows computers outside the LAN to have full access to file servers, shared folders, and network printers within the LAN if they have permission to log on to the network.

reader/viewer A machine that magnifies the miniature images of a microform and displays them on a screen.

reader/printer A machine that displays micrographic images on a screen and that can also print full-size documents on paper.

real A number that can have fractional amounts; 1.5, 3.0, and 4.3453E10 are real numbers.

real image An exact representation on film or in electronic form of a paper record.

record A piece of information created by or received by a business or organization giving evidence of a business decision or transaction. It should be preserved because it would be more expensive to destroy it than to keep it; all the fields about a single customer, stock item, or employee (an example is a customer address record that includes the company name, street address, city, state, zip code, contact phone number, fax number, and Web address).

record locking When the information in one or more records in the database is being modified, the DBMS prevents any other person from viewing the information by "locking" that record or records.

records and information management The creation, distribution, maintenance, protection, control, storage, and eventual destruction of business and organization records. Also referred to as RIM.

records center   A secure location that is dedicated to the storage of all types of documents and records.

recovery   The component of retrieval in which borrowed records are returned.

recycle   To manufacture paper and other products from waste, scrap, used paper, and other items.

relational database   A database with two or more tables that are related through one or more fields; this field must be a key field.

relative path   Part of an Internet address. The list of folder names you must go through to get to a document once you reach the computer that contains the document.

remote access   A process that allows someone to access a computer or LAN from the outside. Once the login process is successful, the outside person will have access to files, printers, and other resources as if he or she were in the office.

remote login   See *remote access.*

repetitive motion injury   Damage to nerves and muscles caused by constant movement.

report   Output from your database involving many records that can either be viewed or printed.

requisition   A written or electronic request for records.

reservation   A function of the request-handling-and-reporting feature that enables an item to be held for delivery on a specified date.

retention   The period of time records are kept, or retained.

retention schedule   A form that lists each category of record and the number of years each is to be retained.

retinal or *iris eye-pattern recognizer*   A biometric access control device that reads retinal eye patterns or the pattern of the iris.

retrieval   Obtaining filed records for use.

root folder   The directory or folder that is accessed directly. The root is either the point where the file system begins or a physical device such as a hard drive.

SAA   Society of American Archivists.

scanner   Input device that converts printed text and graphics to computer data.

search engine   An application that goes from Web site to Web site collecting information, puts it into a database, and returns document links based on words and phrases that the user wants to find.

self-describing   Embedding descriptive information into a document on the Internet. This information can refine a Web search.

server   A computer that gives information to other computers requesting it; usually a machine that is not used by a person at a terminal but rather one that maintains a large store of information such as files, Web pages, e-mail, or other records and sends a copy to computers requesting it; a computer that holds a company's data and serves all the employees who will access that data from their individual desktop computers.

sharing   Allowing other computers on the LAN to see selected folders and their files located on your computer.

shortcut   A special type of file that does not hold any information but points to another file in the file system. Shortcuts allow computer users to store the same electronic records in multiple logical file systems without wasting space or creating update problems—similar to a cross-referencing in paper files.

shredder   A machine that cuts paper into small pieces or strips.

signature recognizer   A biometric access control device that analyzes a person's signature.

smart card   Compact disk (CDs) about the size of a credit card with a small microprocessor that can change the user's access number within a cycle time.

software   Same as an application; a set of instructions that allows the computer to perform specific tasks.

software agents   See *Metasearch*.

software piracy   The act of duplicating copyrighted software illegally.

sprinkler system   Heat-sensitive devices installed in the ceiling of a building; they turn on automatically and spray water when excess heat is sensed.

storage device   Computer hardware used for long-term storage of electronic records. Hard drives and backup tapes are examples.

storage equipment   Equipment used in storing paper records; includes cabinets, storage systems, sorting devices, and carts.

string   A field type that can include alphabetic characters, numbers, and other keyboard characters; also called *alphanumeric*.

subject filing   Organizing records by topic.

subject-numeric files   Similar to encyclopedic subject systems except that numbers are used to identify the captions.

surge protector   A unit between the computer power cord and the electrical outlet that can reduce electrical current overloads and thus prevent the destruction of data.

tab   Extension at the top of a folder or guide where a label is placed for identification.

table   A group of related records that all contain record design in terms of field names and types.

tag   A special marker embedded in a document. Markers are not normally visible. Instead they describe a piece of text or a picture from the application showing the document; html and XML use tags.

TEMPEST   The name for federal government electronic signal emission standards for computer hardware.

tickler file   Another term for a chronological file.

TLD   Top level domain. The part of a domain name ("com," "org," "net," "gov," "mil," "edu," "us," "jp," "ca") that tells the organization category or country to which the domain name belongs.

toggle   Feature that enables the user to switch, or toggle, between one program and another without exiting either.

tracking number   A unique document number used to track a document sent to someone. It is assigned so that both the sender and the recipient can be sure they are referring to the same document.

transactional processing   A safeguard that allows only one update at a time when more than one person is accessing and updating the same data at the same time.

type   A specification for or identification of a database field that must be identified when the database is created.

uninterruptible power source (UPS)   Unit that provides standby power to a computer system in case of temporary electrical power loss.

unit   Each part of a name that is considered separately when a name is indexed.

uppercase   Characters of the alphabet written as capital letters.

URL   Uniform resource locator. A means of addressing any document available on the Internet. Example: http://www.mycompany.com/company-docs/sales/performance.html

user-designed customization   Feature that enables the user to specify the records structure, search parameters, report format, data entry screens, help messages, and language options (other than English).

virus   Unwanted computer instructions that can alter and destroy data.

virus protection software   Software used to locate and eliminate computer viruses.

voice mail   A recorded message that is transmitted from one telephone to another.

voice-activated access system   A biometric access control device that reads voice patterns.

voice-input computer   Computer and software that enable users to speak into a microphone and thus enter data into a computer system.

waiting list   Feature that places a potential user on a list for records that have been charged out.

wildcard search   Looking for records when some of the information is missing. Symbols called wildcards, such as * and ? are inserted in place of the missing information.

wizard   A tool provided by many DBMSs that allows a user to create a form by following a template and answering questions.

World Wide Web   The Web. A subset of the Internet that is a collection of documents linked together using http.

XML   Extensible markup language. A descriptive language that adds tags to a document to describe various parts of it to a search application. A new technology that may greatly improve records management and information retrieval.

INDEX

Abbreviations
  in business and organization
    names, 55
  in personal names, 52
Access, 7, 87
  biometric devices for,
    204–205
  passwords for, 207
  remote file, 171–172
  rights to, 169–170
Addresses
  alphabetizing, 62–63
  computer, 154, 158
Admissibility into evidence, 25
Age Discrimination and
    Employment Act, 23
Air drying technique, 211
Alias, computer, 109
Alphabetic filing systems, 46,
    73–76
Alphabetizing, 47–48. *See also*
    Indexing and
    alphabetizing
Americans with Disabilities Act
    (ADA), 71
And, in Boolean logic, 191–192
Applications, computer, 103, 106
Architecture of automated
    records management
    systems, 193
Archival management, 15
Archives, 15
Archivists, 15
Association of Records
    Managers and
    Administrators
    International (ARMA), 10,
    17–19
    Eliminate Legal Files
    Program, 71–72
Associations, professional,
    16–17
Atlanta Area Technical School,
    101
Attachments to e-mails,
    120–122

Authentication systems,
    207–208
Automated records
    management systems,
    188–193
  architecture of, 193
  costs of, 193
  functions of, 189–192
  types of, 188–189

Background processes, 190
Backing up electronic records,
    124–125, 165
Bar code sorter, 185
Bar coding, 185–187
Batch processes, 190
Biometric access control
    devices, 204–205
Black-box technology, 207
Boolean logic, 191–192
Brevity in file names, 113–114
Browser, 113, 161
Business ethics, 26–27
Business forms, 41–43
Business names, alphabetizing.
    See Filing rules
Business records, laws related
    to, 23–24
By-product information, 89
Bytes, 103

Capital One Financial
    Corporation, 3
Captions, general, 78
Carpal tunnel syndrome,
    199–201
Case (in letters), 47
Centers and depositories for
    records, 16–17
Central processing unit (CPU),
    103
Central storage, 166
Certified records managers
    (CRM), 19
Children's Medical Center of
    Dayton, Ohio, 33

Chronological filing systems, 83
Citizens' rights and
    responsibilities, 24–25
Civil law, 22
Civil legal concerns, 25–26
Civil Rights Act, 23
Client, computer, 156
Command-driven systems, 190
Communication between
    computers, 154–157
Compact disk recordable
    (CD-R), 183
  backup files on, 124
Compact disk rewritable
    (CD-RW), 184
Computer generated output, 188
Computer systems for electronic
    files, 103–108
Computer viruses, 207–208
Connelly, Patricia, 3
Console emulation, 171–172
Consulting in records and
    information management,
    16–17
Container management, 192
Contracts, 5
Control of records, 7. *See also*
    Access; Security
Conventional systems, 188
Conventions, naming, 167–169
Copy machines, 41
Copyrights, 25
Costs
  of automated records
    management, 193
  of recycling files, 93–94
  of retaining files, 38–39, 91
Country codes, 158
Creating records, 5. *See also*
    Hard copy records
Criminal law, 22
Cross-references, 63, 75
Cryptography, 208
Curtis, Elizabeth, 33
Customization, user-designed,
    190

Data images, 179, 184–187
Database management, 128
Database management system
     (DBMS), 129
Databases, 4, 129. *See also*
     Electronic databases
Date fields in databases, 136
Delivery, 90. *See also*
     Distribution of records
Depositories for records, 16–17
Destruction of records, 7–8,
     93–95
Detectors, 204
Dictionary subject files, 78
Digital Millennium Copyright
     Act (DMCA), 23
Digital signature, 121
Digital video disk (DVD), 184
Directories
     electronic, 107–109
     network, 174
Disasters, 208–211
Disintegrating records, 94
Disk technology, 183
Disks, computer, 4
Distributed storage, 163–165
Distribution of records, 6, 87–90
     electronic, 120–123
Documentation
     in file names, 114–115
     of file retrievals, 87–88
     storage, 76
Documents, self-describing, 175
Domain names, 158. *See also*
     Internet
Drives, mapped, 166

Educational records, 15
Electronic access control device,
     202
Electronic Communications
     Privacy Act (ECPA), 23
Electronic database(s), 128–151
     components of. *See*
          Electronic database
          components
     designing, 130–131
     hardware for, 129
     network, 148–149

relational. *See* Relational
     databases
software for, 129–130
Electronic database
     components, 131–140
     examples of, 138–140
     fields in, 131–136
     links in, 136–137
     records in, 137
     tables in, 138
Electronic files, 102–127
     backing up, 124–125
     computer hardware for,
          103–105
     distributing, 120–123
     operating systems for, 106
     organizing. *See* Organizing
          electronic files
     retrieving, 117–119
     security of, 206–208
     software applications for, 106
     See also Electronic
          databases; Network-
          based records
          management
Electronic key, 203
Electronic security card, 203
Electronic vaulting, 210
Eliminate Legal Files (ELF),
     71–72
E-mail, 37, 120–122, 158–161
     for distributing files, 120
Employee Retirement Income
     Security Act, 23
Employment in records and
     information management,
     10–11, 14–21
     professional associations,
          17–19
     specializations in, 15–17
Emulation, console, 171–172
Encyclopedic subject files, 78
Environmental protection in
     recycling files, 95
Equal Pay Act, 23
Equipment and supplies for
     paper records, 67–72
     criteria for selecting, 70–72
     types, 67–70

Ergonomic keyboard, 200
Ergonomics in filing systems, 71
Ethical issues, 26–27
Expansion of filing systems, 70
Extensible markup language
     (XML), 175
Extension, file, 112

Fair Labor Standards Act, 23
Faxes, 36–37
Federal Disposal Act, 24
Federal Insurance Contributions
     Act (FICA), 23
Federal Paperwork Reduction
     Act of 1980, 24
Federal Property and
     Administrative Services
     Act, 24
Federal Records Act, 24
Federal Reports Act, 24
Federal Unemployment Tax Act
     (FUTA), 23
Field definition, 190
Fields in electronic databases,
     131–136
File(s)
     electronic. *See* Electronic
          files
     recycling of, 93–95
     retention of, 91–93
     retrieval of, 86–90
     See also Electronic files; Hard
          copy records
File extension, 112
File folders, 67–70
File formats, electronic, 121
File guides, 68
File labels, 68–70
File names, 111–115
File servers, 169–170
Filing rules, 49–63
     addresses, 61–62
     business and organization
          names, 54–59
     foreign government names,
          61
     names of people, 49–53
     state and local government
          names, 59–60

United States government names, 60–61
Filing supplies, 66. *See also* Equipment and supplies for paper records
Filing systems
    alphabetic, 46, 73–76
    chronological, 83
    geographic, 80–81
    numeric, 81–83
    subject, 77–80
Filing terms, 47
Filmed images, 180–182
Financial records, 15
Find tool, computer, 119
Fingerprint scanner, 204
Fire protection, 70
Fire-resistant storage device, 204–206
Firewalls for computer security, 208
Floor space for filing systems, 71
Folders, electronic, 107–109
Follow-up, 83, 90
Foreign government names. *See* Filing rules
Form design software, 43
Form-filling software, 43
Forms
    business, 41–43
    in relational databases, 144–145
Freedom of Information Act, 24
Freeze-drying technique, 211
Full backups of electronic files, 125
Full-text systems, 188

General captions, 78
Geographic filing systems, 80–81
Gigabytes, 103
Global modifications, 191
Government laws and regulations, 23–25
Government names, alphabetizing. *See* Filing rules

Government records, 15–16, 24
Graphical user interface (GUI), 190
Guides, out, 89

Handprint scanners, 204
Hanging folders, 67–70
Hard copy mail, 35–36
Hard copy records, 4, 34–45
    business forms as, 41–43
    copy machines and, 41
    design software for, 43
    organization systems for. *See* Organizing paper records
    paperwork related to. *See* Paperwork
    retention of, 35–36
Hard drives, computer (hard disk), 4, 184
Hardware, computer, 103, 129
Hayes, Larry, 101
Historical records, 7–8
Human disasters, 209–210
Hyperlink, 163
Hypertext markup language (html), 162
Hypertext transfer protocol (http), 161
Hyphenation, personal names with, 51–52

Identification in file names, 113
Identifiers, computer, 154, 158
Identifying records, 5
Image technology, 179–188
    data imaging in, 184–187
    filmed images and, 180–182
    output from, 188
    scanned images and, 183–184
Inactive records, 7–8, 91
Incinerating records, 94
Incoming paperwork, 36–38
Incremental backups of electronic files, 125
Indexing and alphabetizing, 46–65
    cross-referencing in, 63
    filing rules for. *See* Filing rules

terms related to, 47
unit by unit, 48
Indirect filing systems. *See* Numeric filing systems
Individuals' names, alphabetizing, 49–53
Information systems, 4
Injuries, repetitive motion, 199–201
Input devices, computer, 103
Institute of Certified Records Managers (ICRM), 19
Integrated security systems (ISS), 202–206
Integrity of records, 6, 92
Intelligent character recognition (ICR), 187
Internal paperwork, 40
Internet, 157–163
    domain names for, 158
    e-mail on, 158–161
    World Wide Web on, 161–163
Intranets, 170–171
Iris eye-pattern recognizer, 204

J. Sargent Reynolds Community College, 3
Jobs in records and information management. *See* Employment in records and information management
Junk mail, 35–36

Keys in databases, 140, 143
Keywords, 173, 191
Kilobyte, 103

Labeling backup files, 124–125
Laws and regulations, 23–25, 91
Legal and ethical issues, 22–31
    civil concerns, 25–26
    ethical issues, 26–27
    laws and regulations, 23–25
Legal records, 16
Life cycle of records, 9
Links, computer, 109, 136–137
Litigation, 25

Local area networks (LANs), 156–157, 169–170
Local government names. *See* Filing rules
Locks for filing systems, 71
Lowercase letters, 47

Magnetic ink character recognition (MICR), 187
Mail
  hard copy, 35–36
  opening, 37–38
  outgoing, 39
  See also Paperwork
Maintenance of records, 6
Managers of records and information, 10–11
Manila folders, 67–70
Mapped drives, 166
Mechanical access control device, 202
Medical records, 16
Megabyte, 103
Memo fields in databases, 136
Menu-driven systems, 190
Metadata, 120
Metasearch engines, 174–175
Microfiche, 180
Microfilm, 4, 180
Microform (microrecord), 180
Minimizing paperwork, 40–41
Mirrored, 184
Motorized filing systems, 71

Names
  alphabetizing. *See* Filing rules
  domain, 158
  file, 111–115
  on file servers, 170
  network conventions for, 167–169
National Bank of Blacksburg, 101
Natural disasters, 209–210
Natural language search, 173
Network-based records management, 87, 152–177

accessing information in, 172–175
file system for. *See* Network file systems
Internet and, 157–163
overview of, 153–157
self-describing documents in, 175
Network databases, 148–149
Network directories, 174
Network file systems, 163–172
  access rights to, 169–170
  central storage in, 166
  distributed storage in, 163–165
  intranets on, 170–171
  naming conventions for, 167–169
  remote file access to, 171–172
Networks, security of, 208
Nonrecords, 5
Number fields in databases, 132–133
Numbers, in business and organization names, 56–58
Numeric filing systems, 81–83

Occupational Safety and Health Act (OSHA), 23
Off-site storage, 91–92, 210
Ohio State University Medical Center, 33
Operating systems, computer, 106
Optical character recognition (OCR), 183, 187
Optical mask recognition (OMR), 187
Or, in Boolean logic, 191–192
Organization names, alphabetizing. *See* Filing rules
Organizing electronic files, 106–116
  file names and types for, 111–115
  filing systems for, 106–108
  folders for, 108–109

metadata in, 116
shortcuts in, 109–111
Organizing paper records, 66–85
  alphabetic filing systems for, 73–76
  chronological filing systems for, 83
  equipment and supplies for, 67–72
  geographic filing systems for, 80–81
  justification for, 72
  numeric filing systems for, 81–83
  subject filing systems for, 77–80
Outgoing paperwork, 39–41
Out guides, 89
Output devices, computer, 103–104

Paper, recycled, 95
Paper records. *See* Hard copy records; Organizing paper records
Paperless office, 35
Paperwork, 35–41
  costs of retaining, 38–39
  incoming, 36–38
  internal, 40–41
  outgoing, 39
Passwords, 207
Paths, in Internet searches, 162
Peer, computer, 156
People's names, alphabetizing. *See* Filing rules
Photocopiers, 41
Phrase search, 191
Pointers, 122
Power sources, uninterruptible (UPS), 207
Prefixes, personal names with, 50–51
Preservation of records, 7–8
Principles for naming files, 112–115
Privacy Act of 1974, 24
Privacy of records, 6. *See also* Security

Professional associations, 17–19
Professional profiles, 3, 33, 101
Programs, computer, 103
Protecting records, 6, 70. *See also* Security
Protocols, network, 154–156
Pulping records, 94
Punctuation, in business and organization names, 56

Queries to relational databases, 146–148

Readers for microfilm, 180
Real images, 179
Record locking, 149
Records, 5–9
    centers and depositories for, 16–17
    security of. *See* Security
Records and information management (RIM), 4–13
    automated. *See* Automated records management systems
    employment in. *See* Employment in records and information management
    functions of, 5–9
    legal and ethical matters in. *See* Legal and ethical issues
    network-based. *See* Network-based records management
    profession of, 10–11
    records identified in, 5
    records life cycle in, 9
Records in databases, 137
Recovery from disasters, 211
Recovery of files, 90
Recycling files, 93–95
Redundant array of inexpensive disks (RAID), 184
Regulations, 23–25
Relational databases, 140–148
    forms for, 144–145
    normalization of, 141–142
    queries to, 146–148

reports from, 145
tables in, 143
Remote access service (RAS), 172
Remote file access, 171–172
Remote log-in, 171
Reports in relational databases, 145
Repositories for records, 16
Request handling and reporting, 192
Requisitions, 87
Retention
    of filed records, 35–36, 91–93
    schedule for, 92–93
Retinal eye-pattern recognizer, 204
Retrieval of files, 86–90
    in automated systems, 191–192
    electronic, 117–119
RIM. *See* Records and information management
Risks, 26
Root folder, 107

Safety, 199–201
Scanners, 200
    for data images, 185–187
    for real images, 183–184
Search engines, 173–174
    metasearches by, 174–175
    See also Internet
Searching electronic files, 117–119, 173
Security, 6, 92, 201–208
    electronic backup as, 124–125, 165
    of electronic files, 169–170, 206–208
    in recycling files, 94–95
    systems for, 202–206
Self-describing documents, 175
Server, 129, 156, 166
Shortcuts for electronic files, 109–111
Shredding records, 94
Signature recognizer, 204
Smart card, 202

Society of American Archivists (SAA), 19
Software agents, 174–175
Software applications, 43, 106, 129–130
Software piracy, 25
Sorter, barcode, 185
Standard-size filing systems, 71–72
State and local government names. *See* Filing rules
Storage documentation, 76
Storage equipment, 66. *See also* Equipment and supplies for paper records
Storage of records, 7–8
    central, 166
    computer, 104–105
    distributed, 163–165
    off-site, 91–92, 210
    system, 76
String fields in databases, 133–136
Subject filing systems, 77–80
Subject-numeric files, 79
Suffixes, in personal names, 53
Surfing the Web, 156. *See also* Internet
Surge protectors, 206
Symbols, in business and organization names, 58–59
System architecture, 193
System entries, 75
System storage, 76

Tables in databases, 138, 143
Tabs on file folders, 68
Tags, 175
Tape backups of electronic files, 124
TEMPEST, 207
Terms, filing, 47
Tickler files, 83
Titles, in personal names, 53
Toggling, 190
Top-level domain, 158
Tracking number, 120
Transactional processing, 148
Types, electronic file, 112

Uniform Photographic Copies of Business and Public Records as Evidence Act (UPA), 23
Uniform resource locator (URL), 162
Uniform Rules of Evidence Act, 23
Uninterruptible power sources (UPS), 207
Unit by unit alphabetizing, 48

United States government names. *See* Filing rules
Units, 47
Uppercase letters, 47
User-designed customization, 190

Vaulting, electronic, 210
Viewers for microfilm, 180
Viruses, computer, 207–208
Voice mail, 37

Voice-activated access system, 204
Voice-input computers, 200

Wildcards in records searches, 192
Wizards in databases, 144
World Wide Web, 156, 161–163

XML, 175

Photo Credits

Cover: Index Stock Imagery

Text: Mark Adams/FPG 7; Adjustable Shelving Products Company, Inc. 67; Mark Burnett/David Frazier PhotoLibrary 182, 200(br); Myrleen Cate/PhotoEdit 6; Patricia Connelly 3; Amy Etra/Photo Edit 200(cr); Corporate Express A Buhrmann Company 68(all), 69(all), 70, 74,104(tr); Eastman Kodak Company 180, 181(tl); Federal Express 186; David Frazier/ David Frazier PhotoLibrary 104(bl), 200, 207; Spencer Grant/PhotoEdit 94, 95, 183; Jeff Greenberg/PhotoEdit 181, 185; David Hanover/Stone 201; Aaron Haupt 155; Larry Hayes 33; Bob Llewellyn/Pictor 8; Michael Malyszko/FPG 9; Jeff Mermelstein/Stone 202; Roger Ressmeyer/Corbis 18; Reuters Newmedia Inc./Corbis 209; Jon Riley/Stone 37; VCG/FPG 2, 32, 100, 204; David Young-Wolfe/PhotoEdit 191

CD Instructions

**Professional Records and Information Management
Filing Rules Tutorial
(Windows 3.1, Windows 95/98/ME, Windows NT/2000)**
by Jeffrey R. Stewart

Start-up

1. Insert CD into CD drive and close the tray.
2. Open the Windows Explorer by right-clicking over either the **Start** button or the *"My Computer"* icon and choosing *"Explore"* from the pop-up menu.
3. Navigate to the CD-ROM drive.
4. Copy contents of the CD into an appropriate folder on your hard drive. Be sure that both files are copied to the same folder on the hard drive.
5. Right click over each file in the hard drive location and choose *"Properties"* from the pop-up menu.
6. At the bottom of the *"General"* tab in the *"Properties"* pop-up, insure that the *"Read-Only"* box is **not** checked. If it is, click on the check mark to remove it. Then click *"OK"*.
7. In the Windows Explorer, navigate to the hard drive folder where the files are stored.
8. Double click on the *"FT.exe"* file to start the program. If both files are titled *"FT"*, then double click on the one with the manila folder icon.
9. Enter your name and school name when prompted.
10. At **Main Menu**, make a selection.
11. For help, click on the **Help** button or use the **Help** menu.